Praise for

Major Jackson

"No American poet wears his genius as lightly as [Major] Jackson."
—John Freeman, *Literary Hub*

"Jackson seems to define himself by his eclecticism. . . . His poems are witty, musical, and intelligent." —*The New Yorker*

"Moments of startling linguistic play interrupt Jackson's elegant, semiformal style." —Sandra Simonds, *New York Times Book Review*

"Major Jackson has coined an idiom and music all his own."
—Carl Phillips

"Jackson's adroit lyrics resonate through a kind of fission, the collision of selves and personal histories yielding a most genuine ore." —Gregory Pardlo

"[Jackson's] lush language invites us into the exquisite realms here at our feet. . . . Take it in, be fed, feel close to something elemental again." —Naomi Shihab Nye, *New York Times Magazine*

"[Major Jackson's] poems explore a sense of place that is profoundly human, their vision expansive and generous. . . . Jackson has created a new poetry of praise." —*San Francisco Chronicle*

"Major Jackson's voice arrives with a dissonant, unforgettable blast of perspectives and forms. This is poetry to listen to, to reckon with."
—Susan Larson, *Times Picayune*

Razzle Dazzle

Also by Major Jackson

POETRY

The Absurd Man

Roll Deep

Holding Company

Hoops

Leaving Saturn

PROSE

A Beat Beyond: Selected Prose of Major Jackson (edited by Amor Kohli)

ANTHOLOGIES

Best American Poetry 2019 (editor)

Renga for Obama: An Occasional Poem (editor)

The Collected Poems of Countee Cullen (editor)

Razzle Dazzle

*New and Selected Poems
2002–2022*

Major Jackson

W. W. NORTON & COMPANY
Independent Publishers Since 1923

Copyright © 2023, 2020, 2015, 2010, 2006, 2002 by Major Jackson

All rights reserved
Printed in the United States of America
First published as a Norton paperback 2025

Selections from *Leaving Saturn* (1992) are reprinted by permission of the University of Georgia Press, Athens, Georgia.

For information about permission to reproduce selections from this book, write to Permissions, W. W. Norton & Company, Inc.,
500 Fifth Avenue, New York, NY 10110

For information about special discounts for bulk purchases, please contact W. W. Norton Special Sales at specialsales@wwnorton.com or 800-233-4830

Manufacturing by Lakeside Book Company
Book design by Lovedog Studio
Production manager: Louise Mattarelliano

ISBN 978-1-324-10513-8 pbk.

W. W. Norton & Company, Inc.
500 Fifth Avenue, New York, N.Y. 10110
www.wwnorton.com

W. W. Norton & Company Ltd.
15 Carlisle Street, London W1D 3BS

$PrintCode

*for Sonia Sanchez
& Christina Thompson*

Contents

Lovesick: New Poems (2022)

Let Me Begin Again	3
Making Things	4
The Ocean You Answer To	5
The Sound We Dressed For	6
Thinking in Swedish	7
Language of the Moon	8
Of Wolves and Imagination	10
On Listening	11
It Must Be the Supermarket in Me	12
Poem with Borrowed Image from Marc Chagall	14
The French Quarter	15
Shall Inherit	17
Eleutheria	18
Ferguson	19
Think of Me, Laughing	21
In the Eighties We Did the Wop	22
To the Makers	23
Wonderland Trail	24
A Promise of Canonization	25
Invocation	26
Anacoluthon	27
The Nature of Memory	28
First Weekend	29
Climate	30
Practicing Kindness	31
Memories of West Fourth Street	33

Nashville Sonnet Deconstructed on a Bed of Magnolia Blossoms	34
Ten Album Covers	35
Winter Eclogue	37
Ode to Everything	39
Historians	40
Meeting People on Airplanes	41
Urban Renewal	42
lxxviii. I treasure any man who fashions his walk	42
lxxxi. Pine shadows on snow like a Jasper canvas	43
xciii. The dead are a reservoir of secrets which they horde	44
cxii. Over and over again I bring the peach to my mouth	45
Lovesick	46

FROM *Leaving Saturn* (2002)

Urban Renewal	49
i. Night Museum	49
ii. Penn's *greene countrie towne* uncurled a shadow in the 19th century	50
iii. You are almost invisible in all this plain decay	51
iv. From the Liberty Bell's glass asylum	52
viii. Woofers stacked to pillars made a disco of a city block	53
ix. Bless your hallowed hands, Sir, and their paternal blues	54
xii. North of Diamond Lake, the Cascades, crossmarks	55
Mr. Pate's Barbershop	56
Euphoria	58
Blunts	60
Some Kind of Crazy	61
Pest	63

Rock the Body Body	64
Oregon Boogie	68
Leaving Saturn	70
A Joyful Noise	73
Crossing Over	75
Between Two Worlds	78
I'll Fly Away	80
How to Listen	82
Indian Song	83

FROM *Hoops* (2006)

Selling Out	87
Hoops	90
Urban Renewal	99
xvii. What of my fourth-grade teacher at Reynolds Elementary	99
xviii. How untouchable the girls arm-locked strutting	100
xix. That moment in church when I stared at the reverend's black	101
from Letter to Brooks	102
Fern Rock	102
Olney	106
Logan	110
Wyoming	113
Hunting Park	118
Erie	122
Cecil B. Moore	126
Spring Garden	130

FROM *Holding Company* (2010)

Picket Monsters	135
Creationism	136

Going to Meet the Man	137
Mondes en Collision	138
Migration	139
After Riefenstahl	140
Roof of the World	141
Greek Revival	142
Said the Translator	143
Jane Says	144
Lost Lake	145
I Had the Craziest Dream	146
Life during Wartime	147
Dynagroove	148
New Sphere of Influence	149
Towers	150
Anthrodrome	151
Heaven Goes Online	152
Manna	153
The Door I Open	154
Designer Kisses	155
Fever	156
Lorca in Eden	157
On the Manner of Addressing Shadows	158
Treat the Flame	159
Periplum	160
Leave It All Up to Me	161
Forecast	162

FROM ***Roll Deep*** (2015)

Reverse Voyage	165
Urban Renewal	168
xxi. Greece	168

xxii. Spain	171
xxiii. Brazil	174
xxiv. Kenya	175
xxv. Italy	177
On Disappearing	180
Mighty Pawns	182
Stand Your Ground: A Double Golden Shovel	183
Thinking of Our Shame at the Gas Pump	184
Aubade	186
Special Needs	188
Night Steps	189
On Cocoa Beach	190
Enchanters of Addison County	191
Energy Loves Here	192
Why I Write Poetry	196

FROM *Absurd Man* (2020)

Major and I	201
You, Reader	203
The Flâneur Tends a Well-Liked Summer Cocktail	204
Going into Battle	205
The Flag of Imagination Furled	206
November in Xichang	207
My Children's Inheritance	211
A Brief Reflection on Torture near the Library of Congress	213
The Cloistered Life of Nuns	214
My Son and Me	216
I've Said Too Much	218
The Body's Uncontested Need to Devour: An Explanation	219

Vermont Eclogue	220
Winter	221
Dear Zaki	222
In Memory of Derek Alton Walcott	227
The Romantics of Franconia Notch	232
Urban Renewal	233
xxvi. Washington Square	233
xxvii. Thinking of Frost	234
xxviii. Paris	235
xxix. North Philadelphia	236
xxx. Fish & Wildlife	237
xxxi. Double View of the Adirondacks as Reflected over Lake Champlain from Waterfront Park	238
xxxii. The Valkyrie	239
The Absurd Man Suite	240
The Absurd Man at Fourteen	240
Augustinian	241
The Most Beautiful Man Never Performs Hard Labor	242
The Absurd Man on Objet Petit A'	243
Oracle & Prophecy	244
How to Avoid a Crash	245
Our Eyes Are Far Away	246
The Absurd Man in the Mirror	247
Now That You Are Here, I Can Think	248
The Absurd Man Is Subject to Pareidolia	249
Nothing to See Here, Move Along	250
Double Major	251
Acknowledgments	253
Index of Titles & First Lines	257

Lovesick

*New Poems
(2022)*

Let Me Begin Again

Let me begin again as a quiet thought
in the shape of a shell slowly examined
by a brown child on a beach at dawn
straining to see their future. Let me begin
this time knowing the drumming in my dreams
is me inheriting the earth, is morning
lighting up the rivers. Let me burn
my vanities: old music in the pines, snifters
of scotch, a day moon like a signature
of night. This time, let me circle
the island of my fears only once then
live like a raging waterfall and grow
a magnificent mustache. Let me not ever be
the birdcage or the serrated blade or
the empty season. Dear Glacier, Dear Sea
of Stars, Dear Leopards disintegrating
at the outer limits of our greed: soon we will
encounter you only in motivational tweets.
Reader, I should have married you sooner.
This time, let me not sleep like the prophet who
believes he's seen infinity. Let me run
at breakneck speeds toward sceneries
of doubt. I have no more dress rehearsals
to attend. Look closer: I am licking my lips.

Making Things

Suddenly I had to skewer all my prayers
and slow-roast them in
the open-air kitchen of my imagination.
I had to shovel fire into my laughter
and keep my eyes from blinking. I had to fuss
like a cook simmering storms.
I had to move like a ballet dancer but without the vanity
and self-consciousness of tradition.
I had to blur my scars so I could write into time,
and carry the sensation of walking like a morose
and heavy American sporting a yellow ascot
over Pont Saint-Michel. I want to be
all razzle-dazzle before the dark-cloaked one
arrives for a last game of chess.
My font of feelings is a waterfall and I live
as if no toupees exist on earth or masks that silence
the oppressed or anything that does not applaud
the sycamores' tribute to the red flame like the heat
beneath my grandmother's heart who never raised a ghost
but a storm. So, look at me standing on the porch laughing
at the creek threatening to become a raging river.

The Ocean You Answer To

The letter had not been sung
and the fire not yet delivered.
The traffic light caressed your thoughts and waited patiently.
Sunlight sizzled with onions and two tablespoons of olive oil
and a dark skillet yearned for its splash of garlic. All was still.
Unseen, many marveled in the comfort of their tiny utopias.
But you stood like music with your breath outstretched
waiting for eternity to enter your arms.
Some thought: this is the moment before the undertow of our
    lives.

Only a few considered the artist on her way to a first brushstroke,
or the prayer that would last like a comet
or the smile that reached the hand on a beloved's hip.
Sunlight like golden leaves close to falling put you in the mind of
    Christo
and Jeanne-Claude and the trailing swath of saffron rivering
above your head.

The ocean you answer to possesses a hint of infinity
like a neckline,
like crosscurrents in June.
Only the withered and lonely did not feel the fire.

The Sound We Dressed For

We heard salvation
breaking over the highways.
We cared little of moderation.
We walked into bars and clubs like matadors
and never believed the songs would go
out of us. We pictured the night sky's slow march.
Orpheus gave us courage
especially in Brazil. Enraged at cages,
endless speeches of rain carved us.
Seeing the word *award*, we thought awkward.
We understood the surrealists. Pencils
rained in our dreams like prologues.
We were a gift for the believers.
We erupted appropriately at concerts and readings
and, like de Chirico, we clapped for
the mannequins' takeover, their balanced
hugs and flight. I said to myself: someday
I will no longer follow this reedy band of defiance.
Someday I will sculpt myself out of stone.
I will get past all this singing.

Thinking in Swedish

I could sit the rest of my life
listening to Aretha and pretend
to be an oracle and maybe get a handle
on members of Congress who arrived
squeaky-clean with valiant notions
of purifying the land thick with bribes,
but erred and fell off walls to become
an abandoned prairie of Humpty's.

I have forgotten my escape routes,
the oaks and sequoias, and live
as though sugar were my only stimulant.
I am not myself this morning.
I anticipate the journey to work
as a voyage over seven seas. The teakettle

whistles on about Puritanism
but my insides are tender as a cocktail party
with no one present. I've a peacoat pilling
in a dark closet and the arrow points
due north where I must go but first
tell me about the promiscuous fountains
in Sweden and how they remind us
of the poets and all their animal sorrow.

Language of the Moon

As a child I wanted as many letters
in my bloodstream as the planet Mercury
would allow, and so traveled the city
on buses late afternoons, and read all the billboards
high above the streets and byways,
on sides of factories and churches, and never
heard the sermons of the displaced
or blustery talk of founding fathers, and saddened
when a route snaked through long tunnels,
and then eased when reemerged
out of the murder of light.

I could feel my veins thicken like the winnings
of a Powerball, and the mystery of women
lounging around a gray-bearded man in a silk
smoking jacket drinking a tumbler of cognac
was like the easeful glide of a narcotic dream.
My mouth puckered whenever lemon-colored
arches appeared five stories above the city
like golden gates to an unforeseen heaven.

As a rule I never glanced at other commuters
or curators in loosened ties and tuxedos
who clutched brown-papered bottles
and nodded to a stillness as though murdered in a film.
Instead, I glimpsed myself looking out a window,
awed by Cartier timepieces and luxury cars
that asked was I hungry for speed
or ordered me to let my body drive.

I ate advertisements like sea waves eating a coastline,
and though my sense of self was as bruised as a moldy peach,
I learned to infrared my longings from the inside
and to tally my suspicions from a distance, and now,
when I read a newspaper, I flutter like a sparrow
at a birdfeeder, and when language spills out
of my skull like a massive cruise ship docked
and towering over a line of ramshackle huts
on an island whose blessed poor gaze up
as though a locker of dollars fell at their feet,
my brain closes and my veins burst
as if pollinating the white face of the moon.

Of Wolves and Imagination

for Barry Lopez

Every so often one has to make a sound
of terrible pain as though in boundless woods
among thorns and berries prowling
through bramble and tangled vines
whose presence is a green fog; one has to leave
one's candlelit dinner at Eleven Madison Park
with its white linens sad as milk and silverware
tenderly laid out like an embarrassment of torture,
and one has to gaze into the chambers of a soon
empty heart and return to the kingdom
of creatures and give up the measured silence
of the respectable whose desire and gasping breaths
dangle as though from a string of floss, all squeaky mirth
and nothing more. Every so often one has to
make a sound like a massive season kept in the pocket,
a beaded amulet for when the temperature lowers.
The imagination is a matinee of memories with a side
of parsley like this one: rifle fire complicating
a bed of wild begonia, which is to say, the skies burn indigo
and your breath can be anything possible,
raucous as a church service or the quiet crunch of leaves,
earth's golden confetti held between palms.

On Listening

If you could listen to my thumbs
then you'd hear the history of oranges,
and if you borrowed your neighbor's corkscrew
you'd hear all her sorrows,
and if you rode your tourist bicycle
northwest along Rue de Lyon arriving
at Place de la Bastille, you'd hear three centuries
of curses, the Jacobins testing their aging throats,
and perchance your eyes widened by love
took in the whole sea that is your beloved's mind,
you'd brush and shake the sands out of her hair,
collect them in your lap then jar the beige grounds
so you can study their infinite light.
You need not enact silence or testify
with a tongue like a yolk with no fire beneath it.
Just let the little grains of your voice blossom
like a crest of pine tops, then eavesdrop on
your blood flowing over sinew and marrow.

It Must Be the Supermarket in Me

It must be the supermarket in me,
all lit from inside, full of wide aisles
and thoughtful shelf-stocking
where you'll find my feelings and
memories. That's why on the outside
I look so ordered and put together.
My inner supermarket contains
an old-world butcher shop
with no trace of the slaughter.
Shoppers arrive with an unfathomable
hunger which I relieve by
offering freshness, quality,
and value. Some are penniless
and can only fantasize, licking their lips
at rows of artisanal cheeses and meats
behind glass display cases, the clothbound
cheddars and goat, at ropes of cured
salami and prosciutto. Still
they taste. I offer free samples
at stations throughout
my supermarket so people will
come to know and like me.
In the produce department,
many test my pears and avocados
for ripeness. In the floral area, they sniff.
Some walk off with my bouquets.
I contain cheerful baggers
who will escort you to your car.
At times, truthfully, I dislike this
about myself, forever accommodating.
I've not always had a supermarket in me.
It began when the church in me

lost its congregation and when
I lost my mother's love to cocktails
and other stimulants. There is no place
for anger in my supermarket. I keep
it in the backroom with a sign that reads
"No Trespassing: Employees Only."
It's a way of being in the world,
a self, full of checkout lines and refrigerators,
until someone runs through me,
knocking down my pyramids of canned
goods, or panic shopping, leaving empty aisles.

Poem with Borrowed Image from Marc Chagall

Most days I am full of spacious meadows,
golden fields of yarrow and lupine
undulating in a vale among free anarchists.
Most days I hold it together like the hairpins
in my mother's head, then
other days it is as though I am floating
sideways in a sour aquarium.

Most days I have the faith of coffin makers.
Most days I sit sidesaddle and blow fire.
Then, other days it is as though I am
in a line of ants disappearing into a half-eaten peach.

Some days I am a scholar of tiny differences
and visit museums where I am a hostage
to the visionaries whose indelible dreams arrive
like ecstatic breezes, especially on the fourth floor
where I stairstep my way to the gilded halls
and peer deep into the still lives of fruit
and water pitchers and pheasants
which remind me, I'm told, of my mortality
except I would have included dishcloths and detergent
next to a carcass of a rotisserie chicken.

All suffering goes this way,
we are poor devils made wise
by the heft of our wrecks. Some days, I scatter
fistfuls of stars out of words.

The French Quarter

Over powdered beignets,
over a demitasse of chicory
near Royal, I came to grips I am the lonely sort,
for I am ever seeking an education,
my head sideways, a book winged
in my hand, its words like a concert,
the fried dough going cold and congealing,
the passing tourists drowned out,
a sullen look on my face. It is when I most
want to make love.

Dostoevsky was a way out of my confusion,
as was Baraka, whom I gave my reverence freely.

Nothing I believed stayed and thus my melancholy
deepened though banjos and clarinets played
all over the streets through late afternoon rain,
Black Bottom Stomp, eucalyptus and live oaks
aging against arpeggio runs.

I suffered a great pity, and the gypsies
were all too quick to augur behind cardboard boxes.
Stubborn cats mewled in and out around café tables
and pigeons sprang from gothic balconies
on the square. If I were one to make concessions

my life was a streak of quandaries and doggeries
with quaint and hospitable inscriptions
on doors, every chapter a tempest or escape hatch
at some back table where I read alone
in faint light, a thin band of gold hops
at the bottom of a beer mug.

It is good everyone is having a good time
on the world's piazzas. I am harnessed in the questions
I have made a home. Were I a character
in a novel, I would be assured change was around
the corner, perhaps a priest careworn like me
in this crowd, who likes driving country roads
in winter while thinking gloomy thoughts.

Shall Inherit

Desperate to learn all there was to learn about
empire, I sought all the hushed men and women
sitting on park benches in the domain
of the blessed and thought again of the executive
looking out over the city from a condo
high enough to rehearse his deadpan
showmanship. I no longer craved
quicksand that was the elite and instead
desired what blue warmth I could gather
around a rusted steel drum and its choir of fire,
there where plastic bags and refuse accumulated
beneath the great conductors of suffering. To experience
Einfühlung, I knew I had only to look with the intensity
of a mystic and let the furtive and quivering creatures
into my marrow and not evade the lovesick
and all their preaching, that I had to let
the innocent refugees line my dreams
and abandon the worm-bound bankers
whose denuded eyesight imprisoned them
in vaults of gold. I blew my nose
and imagined a country of the meek,
a feeling like rosebushes with no thorns.

Eleutheria

So little to say of the iridescent grackles
above the courthouse or the architecture
of secrets below like a fragile vocabulary,
or the inundation of idols when winter thawed,
whatever was hidden out of loneliness.
What if we were changed at least once by nights of rain,
by drunken bees in a glade of tufted vetch,
by the fly-tormented psalms of Blake
edging further into the breath of our knowing?
This is a country with a single dream—
all the counties and all the town meetings and all
the demonstrations amount to a sole creation.
Last night I pictured our shadows liberated from human forms.
We know the color of freedom. I've a face the shade
of maple pressed like an encyclic leaf
in a book from another century no one reads.
I am imagining your fingernails, the great potential
of your profile, how you may never hear the gentlest
parts of my tumbling out of clouds:
sometimes we call it beauty, we the martyrs.

Ferguson

Once there was a boy who thought it a noble idea to lie down in the middle of the street and sleep. For four hours no one bothered him, but let him lie on the road as though he were an enchantment. This became newsworthy and soon helicopters hovered above, hosing his curled torso and thick legs in spotlights televised the world over. Foreign correspondents focused on the neighborhood and its relative poverty as recognized by the plethora of low-hanging jeans worn by shirtless men and loud music issuing from passing cars, which had the effect of drowning out everyone's already bottled-up thoughts about the boy sleeping in the middle of the street; others jumped in front of cameras seizing an opportunity to be seen by their relatives on the other side of town because they had run out of minutes on prepaid cellphones.

The roadkill in the neighborhood, and some on that very block, rodents, cats, and possums, feeling equal amounts of jealousy and futility, each began to rise and return to their den holes, cursing the boy sleeping in the street beneath their breaths for his virtuosic performance of stillness and tribulation in the city. The drug-addicted men and women leaning into doorways like art installations were used to being ignored, but they, too, felt affronted by the boy sleeping in the street and folded their cardboard homes.

For the first hour, he practiced not breathing. For ten seconds, he would hold his breath. And then, he practiced longer sets of minutes during the next three hours until he was able to stretch out his non-breathing for whole hunks at a time. When his breathing returned, it was so faint, his chest and shoulders barely moved; infinitesimal amounts of life poured out of him, but no one noticed. The police cordoned off his body, and after some time, declared him dead because they had only seen black men lying prone on the street as corpses, but never as sleeping humans.

The whole world, eager and hungry for a Lazarus moment,

watched and waited to see when he would awaken and rise to his feet, especially his neighbors with minutes remaining on cellphones who filmed and animatedly discoursed behind yellow tape the ecstasies and muted sorrows of watching a boy sleep in the middle of the street.

Think of Me, Laughing

after Gerald Stern

You're right to imagine me sobbing on the corner
of 6th Avenue & West 4th or raising
a hashtagged cardboard above my head
near the Liberty Bell. You're right to
picture me lying down below the gold-domed
capitol demanding Don't shoot!
It is my annual day of sobbing. What are these
brown hands for if not to bury my eyes in the
ancient rivers of wrongs? And isn't this my consigned
single note in our final piece of music, mindless as a blink?
So go ahead: you and I are once again rehearsing decency.
It is the dream of loving fruited plains that do not love you back.
It is our feet planted in concrete that has me weep.
But, first, give thought to my luxuries, the sunset
I toasted over the Val di Chiana with an aperitivo
in Caffè Poliziano the summer of '15, or give thought
to the promontories of conversation with my father
yesterday in which, among other delights, we discussed
the dignity of eggplants whose purplish tint
reminded him of a great aunt. Consider my love
of celestial bodies. You're better off thinking
of me singing this morning a little Marvin Gaye,
not What's Going On, but I Want You, sultry
and soulful: a one-way love is just a fantasy,
O Sugar! Forgive me for being bound up in the
ecstatic right now. I do not regret my little bout with life.

In the Eighties We Did the Wop

If you end your crusades for the great race,
then I will end my reenactments of flying,
and if you lean down to smell a painted trillium,
then I will cast a closer eye on those amber waves,
and if you stop killing black children,
then I will turn my drums to the sea and away from
your wounded mountains. Who mothered your love of death?
Here is a heart-shaped stone to rub when you feel fear rising;
give me anything, an empty can of Pabst, a plastic souvenir, a t-shirt
    from Daytona.
Here is a first edition: *The Book of Light* by Lucille Clifton.
Give me an ancient grove and a conversation by a creek, charms
to salve my griefs, something that says you are human,
and I will give you the laughter in my brain and the tranquil eyes of
    my uncles.
Show me your grin in the middle of winter.

In the eighties we did the wop; you, too, have your dances.
It is like stealing light from a flash in the sky. I promise:
no one is blaming you. No one is trying to replace you.
You are carrying a tainted clock, calling it *European History*,
standing in khakis, eyes frightened like a mess of beetles.

To the Makers

Nights withering into a forgery of chapels,
I give you lacquered bowls of dried leaves
and the fidelity of prayers. I give you bodies
turning this way and that by kimblewicks,
children at the gates waiting for a revolution.
I give you sun-drenched harbors and sovereign kisses.
That is, a startling afternoon of grace awaits us,
and perhaps, our tongues are lined with more than silver.
We must answer this discomfort as soon as possible,
before the proud men prowl slow as
honey over the ears of wannabe barons,
and root in small towns
and corrupt the curious and humane
whose heads draw back and whose
mouths wait for tranquil rains.

Wonderland Trail

Writing birthed me
and the tropic zones of kindness
and the parables in the eyes
of my ancestors which belong
to the crickets talking in code
off a road in Longmire, Washington.

Once again, I am thinking
of Joe Wood on Wonderland Trail,
Joe who vanished into earth,
Joe with whom I never discussed
the brassiness of tyrants
nor the pleasures of lousy coffee
or the peculiar sensitivity of
the willow flycatcher,
how we are found thinking
with grace.

Blizzards trap light. I have seen
an elysian blue in snow holes
that have bewitched my birth,
but who can discern
where darkness dwells?

Turn the searchlights back on.
A star is missing. The coded
voices of birds thread
our emptiness.
True, all lives fade into a fog—
one of the small mysteries
here in America.

A Promise of Canonization

And though I say here sorrow beguiles me
    I lose no sleep;
and though I say our country's journey is one long rigmarole
    its villages and ridges are succulent and sweet;
and though I say here *Watch me now! Watch me!*
    truly I'm shy as stage curtains, demure as cups of espresso;
and though I quote Wordsworth, Zagajewski, and Dao
    I come from gunshots and beatdowns, raw and dirty:
    The day was mild, the light was generous;
and though I've said in the past *I wear / September on my face, /*
    which is eternal, I treasure, too, June mornings soaked
    in song, July's fevered cauldron wilting us to seared spinach;
and though we say darkness succumbs to the light,
    I've been reading Faust, questioning the morality
    of knowledge: our icebergs and mountains
    auctioned, earth collapsing, human flesh for money,
    crickets barking loud as generals;
and though we say I do unto I do death do on cue,
    I'll forever hold her, a jewelry box in my lap
    full of prayers and stays against confusion;
and though they say world without religions,
    without revelations, instinct effaced by reason,
    I swear I can reach up and touch your laughter.

Invocation

Down here we have inherited an arcade of stars
and want kindness that can stop a bomb.
We want intelligence that survives mutations.
No more rallies of hate. No more stone mountains
just proliferating peaks and the presence
of friends like magical wands.

We want the father in the park running
behind a child pedaling into her future.
We want to turn a corner and stumble upon
the muted concert of two people in an embrace
with entangled eyes. We want to hear
a faraway train whistle cast a spell
on the coming night.

Back in that far-away land we were
nurtured once on a dance floor, blazing
in some tribal purity near some bride,
swirling in sweaty laughter
as we reached for the tips of each other's fingers
streaming their ambient light.

Such were the new births of ourselves
breaching horizons like a sting.

This is not the ending we imagined.
We want to see each other again:
strangers walking through curtains
of rain, storms lighting up pastures.

Anacoluthon

What if the wasteland is in us after all,
our spreadsheets casting shadows
that amount to a defamation of the woodchuck?
What if we held an Olympics based on altruism
where the clearest conscience of greed wins?
What if all the painted nudes suddenly vanished from their frames
in all the museums throughout the world?
What if the holothurian was the most convincing aftermath
of alien invasions? What if essays were required in order
to obtain a driving license? What if a volume of poems were
required in order to run for presidency?
What if when we died all of our secrets were handed
as a printout to our grieving families?
What if our ego was an expression of an inverse
correlation to our sense of justice? What if instead
of food we ate musical notes and plot arcs?
What if our tears were collected over a lifetime,
then frozen and served in sympathy cocktails?
What if Heraclitus's River is made of recycled water?
What if the lord our god decided to bring back
the practice of smiting —— as in immediately the angel
of the lord smote him because he gave
not the people glory: and thus, he was eaten of worms.

The Nature of Memory

Once again I am trying to fall into the light,
twice-broken and knife-scarred, recalling my children
on Long Beach Island, loose sand in Anastasia's dreads,
Langston holding a red plastic shovel
in one hand and the sword-like tail
of a horseshoe crab in another,
shorebirds winging above their heads.

If there is another world,
a poet struggles to describe ocean
mist dissipating over a young father,
distant and lonely, watching
his children's laughter run into the sea
then explode at the edge of the world.

What is my life but a constant entering
into a dizzying churn of days,
ping-ponging like numbered balls
in a glass air machine?
Then, as now like all of us, I was brought here
through a clumsy series of human foibles,
and thus am conditioned to read
the underside of storms edging up a coast.

Someday they too will push down far enough
and learn to unfold the minutes and hours into
one long continuous wave. For now,
I hope they love themselves loud as that day,
light-drunk, kicking up sand.

First Weekend

When my toddler son recent of speech
whom I haven't seen in eight days
strapped in like a copilot from his rear seat
asks *Why's mommy crying all the time?*
I pull out of weekend traffic and press the dash's red
triangle, flashing helplessness to passing cars.
He's bewildered, and so am I. We are
spending our first summer days in a nearby hotel
I've chosen because it has a pool with a slide.
I thought so little of him beforehand,
soloing nights in a darkness I've yet to comprehend,
yet here he is, his little voice, his little fingers
and hands which he cannot figure what to do with,
so he kicks off his waterproof slip-ons
and grabs his soles like he used to in his crib,
rocking side to side, but he's harnessed
and tethered and has to settle for a stretch
of his limbs, tightening his whole body to a fraught
set of tense veins and vessels like the passenger
who has given up on a safe landing, who wants
to know the truth of his life, and so continues
his last questions, sensing mechanical failure,
his voice coming to me out of some future wreckage
Did you hurt mommy? Pierced, I turn off my hazards
and gun into a lane of speeding traffic, eyes
darting to and fro like one trying to read danger up ahead.

Climate

What the heart knows: a ramekin
of warm peach cobbler crowned
with a splodge of vanilla whose slow melting
is the altering of the seasons, the coming
of autumn swirling in a mass of milky orange
sugar; Bach's Sonata No. 1 in B Minor,
its opening movement, a sojourn reminiscent
of December rain or my grandfather, graveside,
alone, his frightened stare into a dirt hole
recalling his errors; the heart knows the spine
as the exquisite corridor to the senses, noodle-like
strands registering the tingling of beach
pebbles underfoot, a courageous plunge into
an iron cold sea or the way you feel when she pulls
her favorite lichen green dress over her head,
rivering her body, a fabric waterfall across the heart
which also knows Orpheus's frantic reach,
Bernini's sculpture, Pluto's ghost white fingers
clutching Proserpina's thigh in the Borghese,
or Serena's shattering swing, her victorious
scream, yet the heart does not know primordial
dangers, wildfires scattering a devil's
dream, hurricane winds drowning castles to make
a sudden skeleton of us all, and why we devour
and swallow earth like vultures on a highway,
and stand round, waiting our turn.

Practicing Kindness

It is wrong of me to speak ill of the whistle pig
or the badger or the Siberian chipmunk who engineers
a complex city of burrows and galleries and pours all her life
into managing her hungers across the seasons,
whose foyer to polyphagic heaven is a fallen maple
from eight winters back off Sparrow Hawk Road,

and equally, it is wrong to demean the long-snouted red fox,
friend of the kolonok and master of her errors,
who lopes down Commercial Street in Provincetown
at night, taking in the gently lit landscape paintings
of dunes in storefront gallery windows or reproductions
of the Pilgrim Monument which strongly favors
the Torre del Mangia in Siena, which had me shiver
upon first sight while driving the hills of a Tuscan
countryside the summer of '16,

and I'd rather not pass a disparaging word against
my neighbor who randomly yells
from his car that I am first to integrate his neighborhood,
which is his way of saying he does not see
our black and brown neighbors, for example, Rumana,
a third-generation Bangladeshi American
who's my physical therapist and lives two blocks away,
or the Hawaiian med student who never fails
to wave on his jog to Love Circle,

my neighbor who has lived in Nashville his whole seventy-five years
and inherited his piece of prime and strongly believes
he is stepping into the twenty-first century
by complementing a perceived upward mobility
while holding up traffic. In great perturbation, I simply yell
over the honking, "Go on. There's a line of people behind you."

Memories of West Fourth Street

Why right now the iridescent blue of that bird
from our walk above Villa Montalvo
coming to me like an omen? I look back
and hear Plato talking to himself about futures
by a cluster of eucalyptus trees. Skullduggery
(or kindheartedness? I can't tell) on a train
platform, some wild chief big longhair type
running Monk's scales. The tune? *Don't Blame Me.*
The swiftest blood-hold when a bailaora does
an adjacent stomp and fans her arms as if beckoning,
infinite light drifting from commuters
hastening home like Vikings. Sometimes
you are disrobed in public, sliding like a glyph
beneath the melody of a man trying to put
a few steaks on his table. You are the next broken
beauty carved by a groove.

Nashville Sonnet
Deconstructed on a Bed of Magnolia Blossoms

In this city no one talks dialectical materialism.
From high up the cranes speak an invincible language.
The trusses extend over pedal taverns and tractors,
joyriding flatbeds of dancing tourists, and it is like reading God's lips.
En garde! she says.

Today I am landscaping, staking light
across my wintergreen yard to get the worm's perspective,
to beg his forgiveness.

I am reaching fingers into darkest soil
pondering the afterlife. A house wren
flouts its surefire code to all this
achy breaky singing

—such intricate phrasing like a compass
behind Giacomo da Lentini's feathered quill pen.
I live in a city of acoustic martyrs
addicted to heartbreak.

Plus, this: even the magnolias, vulnerable each
spring, court a delicious despair, and gift their
cream-colored blossoms like spark plugs for the living.

Ten Album Covers

The future is a blind piano man
fingering some groove out
of ancient beats from the Roman Empire.

I do my best to forget
the pale-faced traveler
of the skies, yet remain a prisoner
to his dusty metaphors.

When I cannot sleep,
I count all my likes.

This morning I read Zagajewski,
who recently vanished into a quantum
of light. My belief in art is endless.

On the kitchen counter, right now:
three sunflowers in a clear vase stretching
the day into a single filament of wonder.

No one knows why sometimes
when reading an epic, the face contorts
into a gold wildfire at night,
thoughts smoldering
over a city.

What I am talking about is my funeral
where all the pallbearers are Yoruba priestesses passing
my body once again through a field of summer.

Our great tragedy, abandoning our accents,
surely, our first religions. Then our great triumph,
returning home years later to retrieve them.

Tack me up on your wall.
I want you to feel this energy,
to which you say, "Piddly."

A fox fossilized in the fingers
of a piano player explodes
into a feverish rift,
drowning Zeus's silence.

Winter Eclogue

> An illumined interior suffering core
> *Alexander Solzhenitsyn*

1

In cities overcoats turn everyone to philosophers.
A cold wind weakens their arguments
yet a sidewalk like the margin
of this white page carries the imprint
of their silent mumblings. A sweatered hound
modeling the latest fashion hastens faster than her

owner to a lobby where a doorman, thumbing *The Ambassadors*
with a fingerless glove, almost waves. The sound
of slush beneath tires frightens tourists checking in
The Plaza, less so, on the drive from the airport,
the already dark. So, they forgo afternoon tea
for cocktails and cheerful gossip in The Palm Court.

2

Snow, like death, equalizes. A vacant
lot in the Bronx is picturesque. Broken windows,
frosted over, give the view of a shaken
globe. A blizzard disfigures a rusted plough
in a pasture the same rate as a di Suvero.
At the edge of another year, a squall

arrives like an eraser. I think of Rousseau
tonight, his Carnival Evening and that startling couple
costumed in deep forest, contrasting the desolation
of barren trees? A cold moon? No, ourselves!
That is: This is the season to go unshaven,
or off somewhere warm if you have the wealth.

3

One feels the ache at the core of one's bones
like a throbbing ghost in the machine—
packaged winds from the polar vortex.
Winter casts us in our private zones
at bus stops, by a fireplace, in café storefronts,
each gaze soft as a revolutionary. Who's to say?

Maybe winter is more than mere allegory
for death or Demeter's pain or the old cliché
of Russia. The Gulag in Siberia may have killed the esprit
of its dissidents but, too, gave the world rancorless poets
which is every commuter on a corner, gently staring as if
to summon inner light on days of darkness.

Ode to Everything

Somehow, I have never thought
to thank the ice cream cone
for building a paradise in my mouth,
and can you believe I have never
thought to thank the purple trout lily
for demonstrating its six-petaled dive
or the yellow circle in a traffic light
for illustrating patience. My bad.
In my life, I have failed to praise
the postman whose loyalty is epic,
the laundress who treasures my skinny jeans
and other garments, and the auto repairman
who clangs a wrench inside my car tightening
her own music. Were my name called and I
were summoned on a brightly lit stage to accept
a little statuette, after staring in utter
disbelief, I would thank my dentist
as well as my neighbor who sits vigil
beside the dying far away from the lights,
and my fourth-grade teacher who brought
down three-taped rulers on my hands
as punishment for daydreaming out a window
during an exam I already completed. Mea culpa.
Now that I know the value of the peaks
across from Flanders Hill, I will forever express
reverence for their green crowns.
I will never fail again to say small devotions for
the scar on a friend's face that lengthens
when I walk into a room.

Historians

I have come to rely on the dark pilots
and their sermons of *Before you were born* . . .
which begin takeoffs on the price
of bread in another age or some collapsed empire,
leaving the telephone poles to pursue
dreams of crucifixions.

Above volcanoes of human emotions,
they lose sight of insects pondering
infinitesimal shadows.
They carry memories of forest floors, of trees
like the sycamores who do not mind
starring in German fairy tales.

When their windscreens are struck blind
with late autumn light, their foreheads
crease and the only way to compass
out of the maze of question marks
is to hand over control of their instruments.
They think a violent sorrow is coming.

They feel trapped behind cockpit doors,
ripping through clouds like scissors.
They long for milkshakes and to giggle
freely until no longer numb.

They curse the pages of history books
tossed into the sea, on wet rocks, those pages
of wily tyrants who enjoyed erasing the will
of the people like soap bubbles.

Meeting People on Airplanes

Not that the white-aproned baker
claimed by flour does not excite a sweet
warmth of conversations in cafes
in Dubuque, Iowa, nor that
the honey-faced cartographer does not
flatten me with her calipers
and rulers, her intense inquisitive
gaze, a pencil trapped between her lips,
she, who tracks our history
of desires, and I am sure the costume
designer at my local theater possesses
a fanatical inner life full of fashions and
interiors from yesteryear, his favorite,
the ornate, sensuous Rococo period
of Louis XV's reign and his chief mistress,
the Marquise de Pompadour, but I have very few
encounters left that leave me in awe,
only the poets whose outsized beds
of language rival Tacitus, the poets
whose mental marathons persecute
sharp-suited barbarians, the poets whose
hungers and gentleness orbit like planets,
who make distant galaxies sing.

Urban Renewal

lxxviii.

I treasure any man who fashions his walk
after the woodcock's sky dance,
and any woman who turns her neck
so that her body resembles a candle, so we'd glance
on all her secret fires and wonder
where do we come from, what fording place,
what delicacies of light the Dutch Masters
caught divining a window or bowl of figs and dates.
We cannot afford anymore Elmer's bayoneting
children on the streets of Oakland or algal blooms
declaring war on the cormorant, or the bad debts
of the Tennessee warbler who has just resumed
on my shingled roof his mortal complaint
of our ingenious takeovers. Hey, are you
blazing like Vermeer's paintbrush? Is Saint
Pedro at heaven's gate begging for your
DNA? Some gentle Roman soldier rasps
his last dying prayer in Camden. Halftime
commercials erase our trample marks.
How do I know you're not climbing the lines
in this poem, folding magic into your heart?

lxxxi.

Pine shadows on snow like a Jasper canvas,
if only my pen equaled the downy's stabbing beak
this January morning, her frantic
chipping, more resolve than frenzy, to make a feast
of beetle larvae, if only my wood-boring eyes
could interrogate the known like pillars of sunlight
through fast-moving clouds scanning the side
of Corporation Mountain where on a distant ridge
white plumes dissolve like theories. I cannot hear
through winter's quiet what's worth saying.
Saplings stand nude as Spartans awaiting orders.
The entire forest is iced up, glistening.
Sealed in its form, the austere world I've come
to love beckons, earth runnels soon resurrected
into a delirium of streams and wild fields. Until then,
branches like black lines crisscross the sub-Arctic.

xciii.

The dead are a reservoir of secrets, which they horde
like limes in invisible caves. The dead
are disciplined and close rank like catenaries.
Occasionally, a night wind pilfers soft words
streamed from their occult of mysteries. The dead
avoid all eye contact yet the light the dead see
is all lantern that taunts and calls them back
across the firmament. They sing at the foot
of myrtle trees and read the classics
evenings in dentist chairs. They smell like
disinfectant. Like us, they open their hooked
mouths to taste first rain, a wide, thick
tongue like a dry countryside. If only we could
see them in between lanes of traffic or cross-armed
in our hallways inhaling our love cries, envious
as our pious hands roam like forlorn clouds.
They avoid graveyards, which make them squirm.
The dead have an incurable habit of thieving
The dead want a vacation from the job of being dead.

cxii.

Over and over again I bring the peach to my mouth,
the peach of thunder, the peach of bare necessities,
the peach of starry consolation, a singular path
of desire along my brainstem, the peach of my enemies
whose slights fly over like poisoned air, dark
as an ink blotter, or like honking geese whose blaring still
I welcome. Look at my cheekbones, wet and sticky
with the juice of living. What arrives as a riddle
to others as cloudy mornings is merely the conundrum
I enter like a raft going downstream over rough waters.
I like going in, even against the odds. I swim
in pond scum. I go to the bank like a pauper
and meditate my future between its alabaster columns.
I want no handouts. My pulpy tenacity perfumes
the air, the peach I sink my teeth into, solemn
as the priest of time, another Lazarus forsaking his tomb.

Lovesick

First, you will need to cross some dark threshold.
I suggest lying on your back
in a pasture of cut ryegrass or in a city park.
I suggest planting an arm behind your head.
You have inherited acres of a night sky
and she is your aurora borealis
and though you cannot see the world's
wild shadows, here she will be, nacreous,
grace wavering in bands of blue-green light,
ribbons of gold neon swimming beneath skin.
You will want to write a long letter to your dead.
You will encounter her mind as a kind of iridescent song,
heroic and dense. You will feel fetched as though
from some polluted river. Her glances will pass over you
like folklore. Do not be afraid. This is wonder
mirroring itself and breaking across your face, endless
treetops in silhouette, knowing looks of your elders.

FROM
Leaving Saturn
(2002)

Urban Renewal

i. Night Museum

By lamplight my steady hand brushes a canvas—
faint arcs of swallows flapping over rooftops
swiftly fly into view, and a radiant backdrop
of veined lilac dwindling to a dazzling cerise
evokes that lost summer dusk I watched
a mother straddle a stoop of brushes, combs,
a jar of Royal Crown. She was fingering rows
dark as alleys like a Modigliani. I pledged
my life right then to braiding her lines to mine,
to anointing streets I love with all my mind's wit.
The boy in me perched on the curb of this page
calls back between blue-sky popsicle licks
that festive night the whole block sat out
on rooftops, in doorways, on the hoods of cars;
a speaker blared Little Stevie above Bullock's Corner Store
awash in fluorescence as the buoyant shouts
of children sugared a wall of hide-and-seek.
Because some patron, fearing she's stumbled
into the wrong part of town, will likely clutch
her purse and quicken pace, I funnel all the light
spreading across that young girl's lustrous head
with hopes we will lift our downturned eyes,
stroll more leisurely, pore over these sights.

ii.

Penn's *greene countrie towne* uncurled a shadow in the 19th century
that descended over gridiron streets like a black shroud
and darkened parlors with the predatory fog of prosperity
as familiar as the ornate plot in a Dickens novel.
The city breathed an incurable lung (TB in that time), trolleys
clanged the day's despair. Workers in cotton mills and foundries
shook heads in disbelief, the unfolding theme caked on ashen faces.
Above mantels in gilded frames: tasseled carriages, silk bonnets,
linen parasols echoing the silence of Victorian evil,
the shade soldered to new empires as steam engines hissed,
and brought this century's opening chapter to a creeping halt.
Step on a platform in our time, the city's a Parthenon,
a ruin that makes great literature of ghostly houses
whose hulking skin is the enduring chill of the western wind.
Stare back down cobbled alleys that coil with clopping horses,
wrought-iron railings, to grand boulevards that make a fiction
of suffering; then stroll these crumbling blocks, housing projects,
man-high weeds snagging the barren pages of our vacant lots.

iii.

You are almost invisible in all this plain decay.
Children's laughter echoing in arcs of hydrant water-spray
knots the heart; those black bathers like Cézanne's
will soon petrify to silence. A chorus of power lines
hums a melancholic hymn, tenements' aching pyrrhics,
doorways and row homes crumbling to gutted relics:
this one exposing a nude staircase, that one
a second-floor ceiling where swings
a lightbulb like your chipped soul suspended
from a thread of nerves. You have never imagined
a paradise, nor made a country of your ghetto,
only suffered the casket a vessel for the human shadow,
only feared, longing for other stones to worship.
Sun dreams the crowns of trees behind skyscrapers.
Here the heart is its own light; a pigeon's gurgle
sings the earth. The eyes of the dead float around us: muraled
Polaroids, street-corner billboards whose slogan
read, "Aching humans. Prosperous gardens."

iv.

> Mama, unplug me, please
>
> *Michael Harper,* In the Projects

From the Liberty Bell's glass asylum,
tourists emerge convinced of a cracked republic,
and for signs further join the edge of the human
circle where you break-dance the bionic two-step.
Democracy depends upon such literacy.
Snapshots. Maps. The vendor's fist of stars and stripes—
She sewed pennants. The public gallery of bronze statues
whose Generals grimace frightened looks
on the darkening scenery. Your Kangoled head spins
on cardboard, a windmill garnering allegiance.
Here prayed those who signed for Independence.
Break beats blasting your limbs to Market,
you're ghostbloom in the camera's flash,
so they call you Furious Rocker, Crazylegs—
The circle tightens like a colony, horse-and-carriages
hemming Olde City to scraps of time;
squirrels pre-tremble then leap to bark.
Tourists ease on shades to enhance the dark.

viii.

Woofers stacked to pillars made a disco of a city block.
Turn these rhymes down a notch and you can hear
the child in me reverb on that sidewalk where
a microphone mushroomed with a Caliban's cipher.
Those couplets could rock a party from here to Jamaica.
Its code was simple: Prospero's a sucker-emcee.
Smoke rising off a grill threatens to cloud all memory;
my only light, the mountainous cones of street lamps.
Did not that summer crowd bounce in ceremonial fits?
Ah yes! It was the deejay, and his spinning Technics
delicately needling a groove, something from James Brown's
Funky President. Then, working the cross-fade
like a light switch, he composed a stream of scratches,
riffs. Song broken down to a dream of song flows
from my pen; the measured freedom coming off this page
was his pillared spell of drums—it kept the peace.
A police car idled indifferently at the other end of the street.
What amount of love can express enough gratitude
for those reformulations, life ruptured then looped back,
def and gaudy like those phat, gold chains?
Keep to sampling language, keep it booming
like Caliban yelling, Somebody! Anybody! Scream!

ix. To Afaa M. Weaver

Bless your hallowed hands, Sir, and their paternal blues.
Tonight Kala grazes a palm over a battered face,
feeling his newborn features in a Correctional zoo.
The shock is permanent like the caged primate
who suddenly detects he's human. A Homo Erectus
stands upright on guard outside his cell.
For the record, good friend, tropes are brutal,
relentless, miraculous as a son's birth. King Kong's
memoir gets repeated on the evening news
like a horror flick, and everywhere dark men
are savagely ambushed. So, when a woman strolls
towards a homeless Bigger, the audience
tenses up involuntarily beneath a cone of light.
This is the work of blockbusters: Kala's groan
twisting on a steel cot, and by morning's sunlight,
your cramped hand. Pages pile to a tome
on a kitchen table; its defense is three-fifths
human, two-fifths man. I await its world premiere;
till then, when one hears of black guards who strike
harder, the brain goes arthritic, tropes proliferate,
and a wide screen blooms with images of heavyweights
whose gloved hands struggle to balance a pen.

xii.

North of Diamond Lake, the Cascades, crossmarks
of yew trees, calligraphic leafblades like credits,—
scrolling, behind the scenes, relegated,
we're lost and drive to a pass snow-blocked.
Listening to This American Life,
the brute scoop broadcast as matter-of-fact,
our lives armed with tears in four acts:
Bonding's like scaling Kilimanjaro. Quite
naturally, love's whacked our ribs to steel,—
so, we're better off shoveling vignettes?
Imagine Auden dear penning anti-sonnets,
reasoning we've relinquished a good deal
of vocation. A frayed-winged hawk squawks
above in piercing kilowatts and anoints these summits
coolly with his feathered blood. What's lost?
the kickback of Orpheus; his acoustics lack
confession, and still we turn and inch downhill
in narrow S's, guided by the compass
below his heart. Suffering in nature, the valley rising
on the backs of roadkill. Darling, how else
do we know we are here? These leaves
pinwheeling are songs I sing both grievous
and bracing; each groan puts us closer to the grave.

Mr. Pate's Barbershop

I remember the room in which he held
a blade to my neck & scraped the dark
hairs foresting a jawline: stacks of *Ebonys*
& *Jets*, clippings of black boxers—
Joe Frazier, Jimmy Young, Jack Johnson—
the color television bolted to
a ceiling like the one I watched all night
in a waiting room at St. Joseph's
while my cousin recovered from gunshots.
I remember the old Coke machine, a water
fountain by the door, how I drank
the summer of '88 over & over from a paper
cone cup & still could not quench my thirst,
for this was the year funeral homes boomed,
the year Mr. Pate swept his own shop
for he had lost his best little helper
to crossfire. He suffered like most barbers
suffered, quietly, his clippers humming so loud
he forgot Ali's lightning left jab, his love
for angles, for carpentry, for baseball. He forgot
everything & would never be the same.
I remember the way the blade gleamed
fierce in the fading light of dusk & a reflection
of myself panned inside the razor's edge
wondering if I could lay down my pen, close up
my ledgers & my journals, if I could undo
my tie & take up barbering where
months on end a child's head would darken
at my feet & bring with it the uncertainty
of tomorrow, or like Mr. Pate gathering
clumps of fallen hair, at the end of a day
in short, delicate whisks as though

they were the fine findings of gold dust
he'd deposit in a jar & place on a shelf, only
to return Saturdays, collecting, as an antique dealer
collects, growing tired, but never forgetting
someone has to cherish these tiny little heads.

Euphoria

Late winter, sky darkening after school,
& groceries bought from Shop-Mart,
My mother leaves me parked on Diamond
To guard her Benz, her keys half-turned
So I can listen to the *Quiet Storm*
While she smokes a few white pebbles
At the house crumbling across the street.

I clamber to the steering wheel,
Undo my school tie, just as Luther Vandross
Starts in on that one-word tune, *Creepin'*.
The dashboard's panel of neon glows,
And a girl my age, maybe sixteen or so,
In a black miniskirt, her hair crimped
With glitter, squats down to pane glass,

And asks, *A date, baby? For five?*
Outside, streetlights wash the avenue
A cheap orange: garbage swirling
A vacant lot; a crew of boys slap-boxing
On the corner, throwing back large swills
Of malt; even the sidewalk teeming with addicts,
Their eyes spread thin as egg whites.

She crams the crushed bill down
Her stockings, cradles & slides her palm
In rhythm to my hips' thrashing,
In rhythm to Luther's voice which flutters
Around that word I now mistake for "Weep"
As sirens blast the neighborhood &
My own incomprehensible joy to silence.

Out of the house my mother steps,
Returned from the ride of her life,
Studies pavement cracks for half-empty vials,
Then looks back at bricked-over windows
As though what else mattered—
A family, a dinner, a car, nothing
But this happiness so hard to come by.

Blunts

The first time I got high I stood in a circle
of boys at 23rd & Ridge tucked inside
a doorway that smelled of urine. It was
March, the cold rains all but blurred
our sight as we feigned sophistication
passing a bullet-shaped bottle of malt.
Johnny Cash had a love for transcendental
numbers & explained between puffs resembling
little gasps of air the link to all creation was
the mathematician. Malik, the smartest
of the crew, counterargued & cited the holy life
of prayer as a gateway to the Islamic faith
that was for all intents the true path
for the righteous black man. No one disputed.
Malik cocked his head, pinched
the joint & pulled so hard we imagined
his lips crazy-glued into stiff O's. It was long
agreed that Lefty would inherit his father's
used-car business, thus destined for a life of wrecks.
Then, amid a fit of coughing, I broke
the silence. *I want to be a poet.* It was nearing
dinnertime. Jesús lived here. His sister was yelling
at their siblings over the evening news & game shows.
The stench of hot dogs & sauerkraut drifted
down the dank hallway. A pre-spring wind flapped
the plastic covering of a junkman's shopping cart
as Eddie Hardrick licked left to right, the thin strip
of glue at the edge of a rolling paper, then uttered,
So, you want the tongue of God. I bent double
in the blade of smoke & looked up for help.
It was too late; we were tragically hip.

Some Kind of Crazy

It doesn't matter if you can't see
Steve's Corvette: Turquoise-colored,
Plush purple seats, gold-trimmed
Rims that make little stars in your eyes

As if the sun is kneeling, kissing
The edge of sanity. Like a Baptist
Preacher stroking the dark underside
Of God's wet tongue, he can make you

Believe. It's there, his scuffed wing-
Tips—ragged as a mop, shuffling
Concrete—could be ten-inch Firestone
Wheels, his vocal chords fake

An eight-cylinder engine that wags
Like a dog's tail as he shifts gears. Imagine
Steve, moonstruck, cool, turning right
Onto Ridge Avenue, arms forming

Arcs, his hands a set of stiff C's
Overthrowing each other's rule,
His lithe body and head snapping back,
Pushing a stick shift into fourth,

Whizzing past Uncle Sam's Pawn
Shop, past Phat's Stop & Go.
Only he knows his destination,
His limits. Can you see him? Imagine

Steve, moonstruck, cool, parallel
Parking between a Pacer and a Pinto—
Obviously the most hip, backing up,
Head over right shoulder, one hand

Spinning as if polishing a dream;
And there's Tina, wanting to know
What makes a man tick, wanting
A one-way trip to the stars.

We, the faithful, never call
Him crazy, crack-brained, just a little
Touched. It's all he ever wants:
A car, a girl, a community of believers.

Pest

I heard the terrible laughter of termites
deep inside a spray-painted wall on Sharswood.
My first thought was that of Swiss cheese
hardening on a counter at the American Diner.
My second thought was that of the senator
from Delaware on the Senate floor.
I was on my way to a life of bagging tiny mountains,
selling poetry on the corners of North Philly,
a burden to mothers & Christians.
Hearing it, too, the cop behind me shoved me
aside for he was an entomologist
in a former lifetime & knew the many
song structures of cicadas, bush crickets &
fruit flies. He knew the complex courtship
of bark beetles, how the male excavates
a nuptial chamber & buries himself—
his back end sticking out till a female sings
a lyric of such intensity he squirms like a Quaker
& gives himself over to the quiet history
of trees & ontology. All this he said while
patting me down, slapping first my ribs, then
sliding his palms along the sad, dark shell
of my body.   How lucky I was
spread-eagled at 13, discovering the ruinous cry
of insects as the night air flashed reds
& blues, as a lone voice chirped & cracked
over a radio, the city crumbling. We stood
a second longer sharing the deafening hum
of termites, back from their play & rest,
till he swung suddenly my right arm then my left.

Rock the Body Body

for Cornelius Eady

I.

One summer night I learned the art of
Breakdancing from a guy I'd only known
As Moon in exchange for algebra lessons
On Mondays. A member of the Pop-Along-Kids,
Moon taught me how to flick my wrist
& make a wave. "Check out The Electric
Boogie" he said & worked like a robot;—
One hand extended, the fingers curling &
Uncurling as the arm joints & shoulders, in one
Fluid motion, followed each other like butterflies.
I half-watched, trying to mimic the simple
Placement of feet, but mainly, I thought
Of all the girls that would soon form a circle
As I created illusions with my body.

II.

Mostly Saturdays, I would pass out
Of sight on the dance floor at Chestnut
& 13th beneath a vertiginous globe
Swirling as if each country were a beam
Of light. But nothing brought me closer
To the body politic than when I thrust
My arms out on rhythm & swung
My torso, pirouette-fashion, doing
The Cabbage Patch! Half of what I knew
Of living I discovered in a disco:
The deft execution of bones,
Eyes, muscles, or something so basic
As keeping in step with your fellow man.

III.

You could be at a gay club with your girlfriend
Who insisted on your accompanying her
So that you might broaden your horizons
& be struck in awe at the elegance
Of movement in a dance you heard someone
Mention vaguely as Voguing. The sight of men
Prancing about like royalty, stretching out
Limbs, pampering their features is enough
To inspire a frolicsome bone in your body & join
The fray. The beckoning voice of a man—
Work & work. Now turn & pose—is enough
For you to believe it's all a conspiracy. But you
Don't fight it. You like molding your face,
Twirling in a constellation of men.

IV.

At 10, I did The Freak with Nikki Keys
In a stairway at the Blumberg housing projects
As the music came to us on the 18th floor
Like the need for language or the slow passing
Of jets. A dare, we were up close, all pelvis
Taking in measured breaths before going down
Like a pair of park pigeons. We could have crushed
Pebbles, thrown fine specks of dust
At the moon. We formed the precise motion
Of well-oiled gears fit to groove. This was three years
Before I would have sex for the first time,
Before I would discern the graceful tangle
Of stray gods, the bumbling dance of mortals.

Oregon Boogie

Khanum, the things we did,
that off-night at The Vet's
when Sister Sledge
issued from the jukebox's

lit dome the darker
rhythms of our native
homes; so, waiving all decorum
maps heap upon fugitives

our bodies made one nation
while in cold pints of pale ale
a couple broke conversation,
toasted our bacchanal.

Half-swaying we met
& our lips splashed
like words over a page's white
shores, the foamy crash

of the lonely heart at work,
my hand coasting up
the valley in your back
arriving at the nape thick

with ringlets I slowly brought
to face & inhaled as you spun
out, a laughing pirouette;
the desert in my heart was gone.

But, what of the province
beyond that empty dance floor,

the single-mindedness
of beating rain, the silent slurs

masked by cups of caffeine,
the half-hearted grins,
that say, *Here in Eugene
it's not the color of your skin* . . .

but all the while making
a fetish of progressiveness.
Along the Willamette,
consciousness thins out

like smoke rings of cannabis,
as the city dances the salsa,
as students sip cups of chai
over bell & Cornel, as henna

designs flake from wrists.
The idea *We are family!*
finds its artificial ghost
in the circle of a spun Frisbee.

At The Vet's Club
your smile wide as a gorge;
others eventually joined
doing the "Eugene Dance,"

a spastic, organic whirling.
A break before the next song,
over the jukebox's neon
face, we leaned, waiting—
Bob Marley wailing!

Leaving Saturn

Sun Ra & His Year 2000 Myth Science Arkestra
at Grendel's Lair Cabaret, 1986

Skyrocketed—
My eyes dilate old
Copper pennies.
Effortlessly, I play

Manifesto of the One
Stringed Harp. Only
This time I'm washed
Ashore, shipwrecked

In Birmingham.
My black porcelain
Fingers, my sole
Possession. So I

Hammer out
Equations for
A New Thing.
Ogommetelli,

Ovid & Homer
Behind me, I toss
Apple peelings in
The air & half hear

Brushstrokes, the up
Kick of autumn
Leaves, the Arkestra
Laying down for

New Dimensions.
I could be at Berkeley
Teaching a course—
Fixin's: How to Dress

Myth or Generations:
Spaceships in Harlem.
Instead, vibes from Chi-
Town, must be Fletcher's

Big Band Music—oh,
My brother, the wind—
I know this life is
Just a circus. I'm

Brushed aside: a naif,
A charlatan, too avant
Garde. Satellite music for
A futuristic tent, says

One critic. Heartbreak
In outer space, says
Another—lunar
Dust on the brain.

I head to New York.
New York loves
A spectacle: wet pain
Of cement, sweet

Scent of gulls swirling
Between skyscrapers
So tall, looks like war.
If what I'm told is true,

Mars is dying, it's after
The end of the world.
So, here I am,
In Philadelphia,

Death's headquarters,
Here to save the cosmos,
Here to dance in a bed
Of living gravestones.

A Joyful Noise

Sun Ra & His Astro-Infinity Arkestra
at Slugs Saloon, 1968

I created a vacuum.
My story is a mystery.
Ain't no way they
Can fill a vacuum.

Never again will
They hurt me. All
I hear is death. You
Can only play what

You feel. I butcher
The classics. I'm free.
I'm black. They call
It avant-garde.

I hate myself for being
In the position of playing
In a territory like this:
I didn't want to be

Here. They say history
Repeats. I'm gonna
Tell them 'bout their
Potential to bypass

Reality. I dream too
Much. I'm not there
As a woman. That's
Where I focus thoughts.

I have to hurt friends
For enemies. Because
Of my ideas. If you're
Going with a master

You have more
Options than
Going alone. I could
Be in Congress.

I did the equations.
I'm not where
I'm supposed to be.
I could be in college.

Two psychics told me.
They should have a holiday.
For musicians talk about
How beautiful. No Air.

No Light. No sound.
No Life. No Death.
No Energy. No
Nothing. I am full of

Hate tonight. They
Don't give me
A dime. They gonna hurt
Their very souls.

Crossing Over

Sun Ra & the American Spirit Arkestra
at the Fondation Maeght, 1970

Death, but not
A death. Half-wit
Minutes, homogenous
Seconds, observed

With open arms,
The way myths end
& encircle you.
On a train to Nots,

I caught a glimpse;
It must have been
This way in Kush,
Amid the Pharaohs,

Cork-bronzed eyes,
Airtight helmets,
Whose stone-bones
Served as vessels.

Mars? Venus?
Not the point!
What but a family
Of Dynasties endowed

With the divine
Cadence to administer
The infinite swells
& ripples of Funk?

What if the stream attains
The music? Does it mean
The end to responsorial
Calls, the shuck

& jive of briefcase
Men, the termination
Of Image Awards?
Or can one museum

Rhythm? Where is
Parker's horn?
In any event, we flaunt
The stuff of old

& modern hipness
As if it were a claim
Ticket. The day will
Come: we will have

Wished the world
Had Cabbage Patched
With us, did The Prep
With as much mock

Capitalistic savvy,
Pee-wee Herman'd
Themselves into stiff
Bouts of kindness.

At moments, when we lose
Parts of ourselves
Even if we know nothing
Of Legba, Oshun,

Obatala, we do know it
Has always been the case
To share the bopology.
How else to explain

A Soul Train line
Or the magic pull
Of The Electric Slide,
So much better at willing

Conformity than the Bill
Of Rights? How else
To explain a people
Willing to groove

The Founding Fathers
Till they sweat abundantly
In nods, shuddering
Out of control.

Between Two Worlds

Sun Ra & His Solar Arkestra
at the Painted Bride Art Center, 1992

Galaxy gowns
& velveteen caps,
A pageant of black
Mummers, fire-eaters,

Flying afrobats.
In the month of May
Arrival Zone USA.
Bongos, bamboo

Flutes, clavinettes.
We cross the stage
Like a rope of knotted
Elephants, shambling

Single file. Tonight's
Probe: Was God
An Astronaut? Sun
Harps, space drums,

Vibraphones. I dream
Of Saturn, my home
Moon, Phoebe, my last
Mission under

Different stars.
I strike the keyboard,
Prelude to Stargazers,
& recall that night

At Club de Lisa's,
1946, a party of white
Patrons pulling back
The curtain separating

The races, Sound
Scopes, Rocksichords,
Oboes. 5 billion
People on this earth

All out of tune.
Minutes from
The cracked bell
I plot a map

Of stars: Ursa Major
To Vine & 2nd & order
This gathering of
Intelligent earthlings

To embark upon tonight's
Spaceship—Ihnfinity, Inc.
Cosmic koras, bassoons,
Sharp, brass trumpets.

Beamed on
The cyclorama, Novas
Moons & Jupiter's
Baleful eye. Cow bells

Wind synths, organ
Music. My Myth
Space Lab, next best
Thing to a crystal ball.

I'll Fly Away

I'm best when I'm running full-throated
towards the whitecaps in Truro,
piping my woeful tunes swell upon swell,
keeping company with the red-winged blackbird
who my ancient friend Gerry once said
governed these parts with his running mate,
the dusty miller. One ruled by land, the other
by sea; one painted the air with swoops
and trills and praised shafts of light,
the other buried himself in sand, imitating tyrants,
cursing the vast tongue of the ocean. This was years
before Henry James and the Mayflower
and the founding of the ballot and years before
Wm. Bradford established his ale house
on Main in Provincetown.

Today I run the shoreline with my neighbor's collie,
blessing his dumb search for wet bark
with a little jaunt of my own, exchanging
dirges of our common dream of flight,
my arms thrown back to lift my capelike towel,
thinking what would it have been like
if there had been no footprints to study
the way back to my beloved grief
if children had not waved my journey
through seaweed and spindrift
if I would have lived all day watching
schooners and barges edge toward Brooklyn,
sipping my sweet glass of tea, dozing off
from time to time, breaker foam lapping
at my tired black feet.

There was never a sound beside the sea
except one and that was my long sigh
the horseshoe crab heard as a whisper
and there was never a shadow sprawled
above Truro large as the one I cast
the retired governor saw as a crow.
Little Orville and Little Wilbur Wright
must have jogged along a beach like this one,
enraged to find no fresh sand to
spike their imprints, and no sea air free
of brine or herring calls or mollusks
or jellyfish, and fallen down beside them,
grieving, as I have on occasion, waiting
for water to come in quietly.

How to Listen

I am going to cock my head tonight like a dog
in front of McGlinchy's Tavern on Locust;
I am going to stand beside the man who works all day combing
his thatch of gray hair corkscrewed in every direction.
I am going to pay attention to our lives
unraveling between the forks of his fine-tooth comb.
For once, we won't talk about the end of the world
or Vietnam or his exquisite paper shoes.
For once, I am going to ignore the profanity and
the dancing and the jukebox so I can hear his head crackle
beneath the sky's stretch of faint stars.

Indian Song

after Wayne Shorter

Freddie Hubbard's playing the cassette deck
forty miles outside Hays and I've looked at
this Kansas sunset for three hours now,
bristling as big rigs bounce and grumble
along I-70. At this speed cornfields come
in splotches, murky yellows and greens abutting
the road's shoulder, the flat wealth of the nation whirring by.
It's a kind of ornamentation I've gotten used to,
as in a dream. Espaliered against the sky's blazing,
cloud-luffs cascade lace-like darkening whole fields.
30,000 feet above someone is buttering a muffin.
Someone stares at a Skyphone, and momentarily,
a baby cries in pressurized air. Through double-paned squares,
someone squints, fields cross-hatched by asphalt-strips.
It is said Cézanne looked at a landscape so long he felt
as if his eyes were bleeding. No matter that. I'm heading west.
It's all so redolent, this wailing music, by my side
you fingering fields of light, sunflowers over earth,
miles traveled, a patchwork of goodbyes.

FROM
Hoops
(2006)

Selling Out

Off from a double at McDonald's,
no autumnal piñata, no dying
leaves crumbling to bits of colored
paper on the sidewalks only yesterday,
just each breath bursting to explosive fog
in a dead-end alley near Fifth, where on
my knees, with my fingers laced on my head
and a square barrel prodding a temple,
I thought of me in the afterlife.
Moments ago, Chris Wilder and I
jogged down Girard, lost in the promise
of two girls who winked past pitched
lanes of burgers and square chips
of fish, at us, reigning over grills and vats.
Moments ago, a barrage of beepers
and timers smeared the lengths of our chests.
A swarm of hard-hatted dayworkers
coated in white dust, mothers on relief,
the minimum-waged poor from the fast-
food joints lining Broad, inched us closer
in a check-cashing line towards the window
of our dreams,—all of us anxious to enact
the power of our riches: me in the afterlife.
What did it matter, Chris and I still
in our polyester uniforms caked
with day-old batter, setting out
for an evening of passion marks?
We wore Cazals, matching sheepskins,
and the ushanka, miles from Leningrad.
Chris said, *Let's cop some blow, despite
my schoolboy jitters.* A loose spread
of dealers preserved corners. Then a kid,

large for the chrome Huffy he pedaled,
said he had the white stuff and led us
to an alley fronted by an iron gate on
a gentrified street edging Northern Liberties.
I turned to tell Chris how the night
air dissolved like soil, how jangling
keys made my neck itch, how maybe
this wasn't so good an idea, when
the cold opening of gun-barrel
steel poked my head, and Chris's eyes
widened like two water spills before
he bounded away to a future of headphones
and release parties. Me? The afterlife?
Had I ever welcomed back the old
neighborhood? Might a longing
persistent as the seedcorn maggot
tunnel through me? All I know:
a single dog barked his own vapor,
an emptiness echoed through blasted
shells of row homes rising above,
and I heard deliverance in the bare
branches fingering a series of powerlines
in silhouette to the moon's hushed
excursion across the battered fields
of our lives, that endless night
of ricocheting fear and shame.
No one survives, no one unclasps
his few strands of gold chains
or hums "Amazing Grace" or pours
all his measly bills and coins into the trembling,
free hand of his brother and survives.
No one is forced facedown and waits
forty minutes to rise and begin again
his march, past the ice-crusted dirt,

without friendship or love, who barely knew
why the cry of the earth set him running,
even from the season's string of lights,
flashing its pathetic shot at cheer—to arrive
here, where the page is blank, an afterlife.

Hoops

for Hank Gathers

I.

By a falling Cyclone chain-
link fence, a black rush streaks
for netted hoops, & one alone
from a distance breaks

above the undulant pack, soars—
more a Sunday Skywalk,
he cups the ball, whirling his arm,
swoops down a Tomahawk.

"Radar! Don't fly without me!"
It's Big Earl who coughs then downs
his bottle, a 40 oz. of Olde E.
Laughter makes its rounds.

I cross a footpath of a city block,
a short rut that snakes between
a lush epitaph of dandelions
& weed-brush behind Happy

Hollow Courts; the ghost
of a staircase echoes here: sign
of lives lived, of souls lost.
Faded hues of graffiti lines

bombed on a wall, PHASE
says Don't Stop the Body Rock.
At gate's entrance, my gaze
follows Radar & his half-cocked

jump shot. All morning I sang
hymns yet weighed his form:
his flashing the lane, quick-
stop to become skyborne.

Elbows posed like handlebars,
he flicks a wrist, the pill arcs
through sunlight glare,
& splashes the basket's

circle of air. A boombox bobs
& breaks beats on a buckling sea
of asphalt;—the hard,
driving rhymes of BDP,

rousing that rowdy crowd
of hustlers tossing craps, waging
fists & dollar bets, only louder—
& one more enraged

promises to pistol-whip
the punk who doesn't pay.
He doubles up, blows a kiss;
each dealer counts his days.

I turn from these highlights—
Spaldings missile like meteors.
Radar dribbles near. "You're late."
Before I speak a word,

"My boy, shootin' geometry!"
We laugh. Father Dave, coach
at St. Charles, once let me
play as a walk-on in hopes

I would tutor Radar. Not even
Pythagoras could awaken
in his head the elegance
of a triangle's circumference.

Four years later, he's off
on scholarship to UNC.
I'm to study Nabokov
at state's university.

Proof of Pop-pop's maxim,
"There's more ways to skin . . ."
If the slum's our dungeon,
school's our Bethlehem.

Yet what connects those dots
that rattle hustlers' palms
with Radar's stutter step
& my pen's panopticon?

It casts shadows dark
as tar as we begin
our full-court run. A brick
off the half-moon's side

—in waves, we sprint.
No set offense: his pass,
my bounce, his deft
lateral, two-hand jam.

II.

Stark Sunday afternoon light,
unending solo of sky,
a parade of leaps
& weaves fortifying

our store of groans, each
glistening muscle surging towards
the body's curative peaks,—
nimble, sprung, absorbed

in our picks, touch, & rolls,
we swerve across haloed
turf whose ceremony overruns
suffering, an arpeggio

of chucks, split-second lobs
past a squad of sweat-backed
ghosts,—pass, glide,
post, pivot away, look

then dish: follow through,—
Swish! Radar backpedals
as the net strings flap & swing to
rest. The blacktop ripples,

raising its curtain of steam;
five ballers grudgingly exit
& make for the next team.
Top of the key, hand on hip,

I point for art's sake, for jest
a finger,—challenge
Radar in a dunking contest.
Just then a car engine

revs Oxford Ave., stalls & peels
out: panther-like Camaro
whose chrome wheels
screech to a stop. Its smoke-

tinted window drops diplomatic-
ally; a frenzied rustling
rising like shrieks fumbling
inside a scream, & the rusted

base of pole where life
snakes an open cut
up to center court, there lay
Radar enfolding his heart.

III.

The ceiling in my room
a projector's canvas, the moon
a flurried cone of light
to which I recite Brooks,

Frost, Hughes. Lying back
in my mind, each book's
a slide held up like a snap
-shot, giant stills illumined

by that Cyclops's eye.
Below bunk my cousin
stacks tens, twenties,—
pacing corners till twelve,

he & the Ooh-mob Gang
slinging plastic vials
of crack, the cursed slang
of death: "I'm gonna buy

a Gucci watch, Air Nikes,
the hypest gear to look Fly."
dazed he says then cocks
a Wesson; what spells

in the ovals of dead
men's eyes? Other circles
festoon above my head,
O's on the tongue

& bitter to the edge:
"We / Die soon."
A darkness spreads—
at first as clouds float-

ing like this craft's spirited
march, then arise
faces of friends resting
in caskets: Deshaun,

Darnell, Lil Mike,
Shantel, a slideshow
whose carousel double-quick
click ricochets shots

across this elegiac. Gazing
its portraits I muse, "This
ceiling's more their grave,"
then lower my eyes to toss

my grief on the shelf of their
sinking coffin, beside
that lone rose laid for dear
parting & hear rise from earth

the hurt motto bred
(as my pen's pitch of dirt
pyramids my dread):
"Fuck tomorrow; that's

how I'm living kid. Fuck
tomorrow." It was Tupac
on the waves: Thugged
to Life. By song's end,

he's martyred again.
My cousin lounges back
inside the rap's refrain,
fingering his square sack

of spliff. He lip-syncs
his resurrected lyrics.
His pain shrinks to
drags of dialect.

IV.

A morning truck grates
by grinding waste;
a bus at the corner hisses,
and so Radar, life erases.

Overnight a muralist
bombed a portrait,
your Daily News All-City
dunk. Inside the pill: R.I.P.

& the too few years hemmed
between the cupped hands
of parentheses. Children mosey
like indifferent supermen

passing the liquor storefront.
The leastwise drunks
line up as if for a wage,—
the state unrolling its cage.

With nowhere to go,
a cortege of souped-up low
riders blares up the street.
A rapt motorcade beats

the crew cool inside alone,
head-nodding their own
extinction. All's blasé.
What use the phrase *Tolle*

et lege or the graffiti artist's
heroic tags? A sneaker's a cave.
The legions of lines my fist
inscribes call back your days.

Urban Renewal

xvii.

What of my fourth-grade teacher at Reynolds Elementary,
who weary after failed attempts to set to memory
names strange and meaningless as grains of dirt around
the mouthless, mountain caves at Bahrain Karai:
Tarik, Shanequa, Amari, Aisha, nicknamed the entire class
after French painters whether boy or girl. Behold
the beginning of sentient formless life. And so,
my best friend Darnell became Marcel, and Tee-tee
was Braque, and Stacy James was Fragonard,
and I, Eduard Charlemont. The time has come to look
at these signs from other points of view. Days passed
in inactivity before I corrected her, for Eduard was
Austrian and painted the black chief in a palace in 1878
to the question whether intelligence exists. All of Europe
swooned to Venus of Willendorf. Outside her tongue,
yet of it, in textbooks Herodotus tells us of the legend
of Sewosret, Egyptian, colonizer of Greece,
founder of Athens. What's in a name? Sagas rise and
fall in the orbs of jump ropes, Hannibal grasps a Roman
monkey bar on history's rung, and the mighty heroes at recess
lay dead in woe on the imagined battlefields of Halo.

xviii.

How untouchable the girls arm-locked strutting
up the main hall of Central High unopposed
for decades looked. I flattened myself against
the wall, unnerved by their cloudsea of élan, which
pounced upon any timid girl regrettably
in their way, their high wattage lifting slow motion
like curls of light strands of honey. The swagger
behind their blue-tinted sunglasses and low-rider
jeans hurt boys like me, so vast the worlds
between us, even the slightest whiff of recognition,
an accidental side glance, an unintended tongue-piercing
display of Juicy Fruit chew, was intoxicating
and could wildly cast a chess-playing geek into
a week-long surmise of inner doubts, likelihoods,
and depressions. You might say my whole life led
to celebrating youth and how it snubs and rebuffs.
Back then I learned to avoid what I feared
and to place my third-string hopes on a game-winning
basketball shot, sure it would slow them to a stop,
pan their lip-glossed smiles, blessing me with their cool.

xix.

That moment in church when I stared at the reverend's black
kente-paneled robe & sash, his right hand clasping the back
of my neck, the other seizing my forehead, standing
in his *Watch this* pose, a leg behind him ready to spring,
his whole body leaning into the salvation of my wizened soul,
I thought of the Saturday morning wrestlers of my youth who'd hold
their opponents till they collapsed on a canvas in a slumberous
heap, and how it looked more like a favor, a deed, though barbarous,
a graceful tour out of this world, that chthonic departure
back to first waters, and wondered what pains I endured
in Mr. Feltyburger's physics class, worshipping light, density, mass,
preferring to stare long at snowdomes or the carcasses
of flies pooling above in the great fluorescent cover, and how beds
are graves, my mother and father kissing each other's head,
their cupped faces unhurriedly laying the other down,
and how all locked embraces light in my mind from below
in blue neon like you'd find on the undercarriage of sports cars,
and then what came was the baker stacking her loaves,
one by one, into little coffers, and Desdemona's
last surrender to Othello's piercing glance, and Isaac shown
a militia of clouds over Moriah, and the dying we submerge
in a baptism of pillows, and how we always loiter at this verge,
there, between rising up and falling back, as in now, this tank
of sound I swim in, gripped between the push and yank
of his clutch, caught in that rush of tambourines next to solemn
trays of grape juice and bits of crackers held by deacons when
the reverend, serious as a pew, whispered, "Fall back, my son. Fall."

From *Letter to Brooks*

Fern Rock

Dear Gwendolyn—or is it Dear Madam?
 Or as Quraysh would more likely say,
Mama Gwen. He, unlike orphaned Adam,
 Had you no less arriving to the fray,
 That surrogate mentor-friend who pays
Art's admission fee. Only since your absence
Our tour's been self-guided. Anthologists

Disagree, respectfully of course—for what
 Is a corpus but the Spirit on foot?
On such ground I begin my epistolary chat,
 Although I gather you'd prefer we strut
 On through, fisted pens raised imaging truth.
Plus up there you must I bet have other
Celestial errands with which to bother.

I consulted Langston my son on this point
 Who thought you now in charge of lyres
& harps, tuning strings, adorning joints—
 An answer he imagined I'd like to hear,
 The professorial poet whose overbear-
Ing view, children best fulfill dad's dreams,
Thus prove black laureates lurk in the genes.

How vain, too, parents who schedule
 A child's every waking hour: from ballet
Instruction to sailing camps to, as usual,
 A learning of the scales. Horseplay's
 For the under-classed lazy. I've heard say

Mattel is to market kiddy PalmPilots,—
Or was it (oh, shoot!) laptops for tots?

I write from Colorado at my desk
    In the Magnolia Hotel. This week's
Poet-in-residence, I feel Audenesque,
    Having traveled this far to mount & speak
    On the habits of my muse or to critique
Student poems, staying mostly honest,
Till a line, like this, begets cardiac arrest.

I should have donned an oxygen mask;
    Breathing here comes in fits and starts. Last
Night, reciting poems, between words, short intakes
    Of breath which made their stress lusty,
    Urgent, a collage of gasps as if life
Were panting out like a morning glory
In the end, tight-lipped, a memento mori.

My hosts are cheerful, delighted I've come
    The distance. They stomach my eccentric
Air, regard me a linguistical phenom.
    Who sports floppy hats and eats carrot sticks,
    Speaks in non sequiturs more to affix
The idea they're getting their money's worth:
Platonic poet heads above planet Earth.

I'll dash this note off promptly; I've checked
    My itinerary. I'm off on a visit
To North Denver High and to be picked
    Up any minute. The unseen benefits
    Of words I'll promote. On cannabis
I'll be most emphatic, "Kids, deign to avoid.
You'll likely catch the paranoids."

I take my cue, as you have likely guessed,
    From the recent bloom of epistles.
Doty's "Letter to Walt Whitman," his largesse
    Of fraternal pluck, make many an apostle.
    But several reads after, the muscle
Of Auden's eye had me finally concede
One's growth relies on one's gift to exceed

One's reach. So, I hope this note is welcomed,
    Your kindnesses being legendary,
Death failing to place a moratorium
    On poets' fan mail, yours especially.
    Michael S. Harper et al. brazenly
Claim your work eminent among the boys,
Your pen's the equal of Chaucer, Dante, Joyce.

Reprints assure postal bins stay full.
    You're not likely to receive death threats.
Be wary wax-sealed envelopes bearing skulls.
    A deaf critic is a cause for fret,—
    Albeit doubtful packages of anthrax
Should arrive at heaven's pearly gates,
Doubtful, too, Hugh Hefner & his playmates.

I contemplated sending by email.
    We've gone gaga over the Inbox.
Each in his cell blinking forward fulfills
    Globalism's promise: round-the-clock
    Friendships; a forum for every boycott.
Electronic petitions are a bit of a drag.
How many times will the NEA be bagged?

Thousands of fingers, even now as I write,
    Draw near the keyboard's ENTER key
In hopes of keeping at bay the strange sight
    Of their faces reflected in the screen
    Or the dreadful lie that life is but a dream:
The mean world seen through the inflated tear
Callous enough to ignore our reckless fears.

Olney

Why write to you? I cannot envision
    A more enigmatic woman who demands
Greater attention, so many questions
    Linger. I thought of you in Ireland
    While biking the countryside, my hand
Swept aside a delicate mist of longing,
And I saw myself with my childhood gang

On the stoop where we played Hearts for dimes,
    Slap-boxed, or simply posed against a ride,
Crotch-cupping. Those lush green Irish plains
    Fell on the upclimb, yet the expanse was wide,
    So I suffered the exile's self-afflicting, evil-eyed
Probe. I would have felt as alien in Sierra Leone.
What was I doing so far from home?

I recalled at once your well-spun phrase:
    "Puzzled wreckage / Of the middle passage."
Bewilderment bores, true—still, amazing:
    Your lines give weight to baggage.
    Art's doing is to lift the sheet off the cage;
The psychic wounds within rendered bite-sized,
Pertinent, grave: our selves no longer disguised.

The next pub I chose I raised a dark pint,
    Then another: to you and my acute
Isolation, to the hoodwinked, the Niña, the Pinta,
    & Sinterklaas, to my urban canticle,
    To Yeats, to rugby, to British cutlasses,

To clean-shaven heads and black Doc Martens,
To stampeding hoofs rounding the margins,

To flags of fear I raised in Skibbereen,
    To nationalists in Belfast, Donegal, and Dublin,
To tweeded tourists, to middle-class imaginings
    Of coats of arms where heraldry gilds the skin:
    Bobo out of paradise wears Ralph Lauren,
To bagpipes soothing the American caste,
To class ascension and dignified pasts;

To Ireland and its convincing show
    Of ale and class, & self-conceptions
That bruise, to our vulnerable muse, kow-
    Towing to the times. Let's take exception
    To decrees where aesthetics né precepts
Based on continents, eye colors, or looks
Produce poems whose centers go uncooked.

The bar empty, I surveyed the length
    Of my bottle, outside the pastoral view.
What I longed for? The medicinal imprint
    Of skyscrapers, the proverbial tennis shoe,
    A power line, or night pavements which knew
My mind's folds. But, no Carl Orff given
To drinking songs, I learned to enliven

The *Luftmensch* in me. Mornings I visit
    The sports page to learn last night's score.
My car radio's tuned to Top 40. I commit
    To memory Oscar nominees, for
    The age underlooks its importance,—nor
The Sunday crossword would I likely complete
If I could not name the king of popular beats.

Fukuyama got it right: we've reached
    The end of poetry (smart reader: allow
In earnest this fallacy). The last man's deep-
    Seated longings having evolved, now
    Prefab his urges and feelings which bow
To set stimuli hurtful as fast-food close-ups:
Styrofoam hash browns, billboard coffee cups.

Yet, explain it thus: remembrance of life
    Summoned in a stroke or song or delivered
In a few lines of verse should somehow lift,
    Steady us more: the meandering river,
    The embraced body held as it shivers,
A waning sky, a fiery scream at dusk,
Baked blueberries spilling from a pie crust.

No doubt you'll pardon these digressions,
    Enjoying a life absent of hours to read.
Detours add to a sightseer's possessions.
    We're all the richer when artists feed
    The mind's thirst with things to see than proceed
Like a train between points A & B, never out
To explore as many views to talk about.

Although the Rockies do not picture
    Firm in my window, I'm aware they're there—
White peaks cresting gives texture
    To rose-light dusting the sky. I stared
    On my way here and turned my cab fare
To a docent's fee, having asked the long
Ride in. A sutured horizon stretched along,

& my guide, a man hacking through phlegm,
    Gestured with his head, "That's Columbine."
& hacked again, his soundtrack to the cam
    Capturing bodies slayed by bombs & Tec-9s
    As if the allegory of living were the crime.
We must not speak it: we're doomed to playact
Our outlaw past. Our psychopathic,

Trenchcoat children whisper in civics class
    The 2nd Amendment like the fate
Of a prayer, then open fire en masse—
    In combat protecting the state
    From aliens? On a murderous march of hate,
Our genetically enhanced super-soldiers
Leave bodies for dead: Martians, human, deer.

The light's blinking red on the telephone,
    Which means I've likely missed my summons.
My escort awaits. I'll have to postpone,
    Pack my shoulder bag, make it on the run.
    Before I jet though, let me list off, one
By one, potential postmarks from various states—
Oh, I should just go. I'm dreadfully late.

Logan

A halyard peals and resounds this clear morning
    Over Torch Lake. Its empty clang
Accents the joy I feel by contrast.
    Dithering Heights is what we've come to name
    The in-laws' summer, Bellaire home. The aim
Here, to rest as hard as you can, or race in as
Many of the club's sailing regattas.

I stay dockside, but on occasion will crew.
    Being as I have as much experience
As flying a plane, there's not much for me to do,
    Except duck when we tack lest I'm knocked past
    Tense. I prefer to watch from a distance
With a chilled glass of white. My feet propped up
As Big Jim maneuvers to win the cup.

The beauty of the angled sails pacing
    On the horizon I liken to
A covey of Brancusi's *Bird[s] in Space*,
    Thus supporting Levi-Strauss's view
    The signified and signifier breaking in two,
Abstraction speeds up the divorce;
O, the pleasures of a conceptual horse.

You were the Empress of the Portrait. Take
    "The Sundays of Satin-Legs Smith." Abiding,
Pimped-out now princely in gold, he pulsates
    In splashes of music videos, a glittering
    Sham, wrists thrust out, diamond bling

His need, sparked by an inner charge to adorn—
Visibility he seeks, thus a man to scorn.

The black intellect is no different, is she?
    Baldwin's fierce saunter up rue de Verneuil,
Petal collar blazed up flashed fain Paris,—
    Too shadowy here, Saint Germain's vernal
        Blossoming of café dwellers became art's infernal
Jamboree of brains where Wright and Himes
Stylized, too, their sidewalk stares, making them

Super-luminal, the modernist trick
    Of burnishing—self-exile, the gold tooth
In the cerebral's mouth. Pound flipped
    In a Venetian recording booth;
        Wystan traded faded Albion for youthful
Guys on 52nd; a Parisian atelier
Christened Radnitsky Man Ray.

Rare is the change of Leroi in Cuba
    To Black Magic Imamu to Amiri,
Vitriolic critic of the petit bourgeois,
    Who caught Fidel's fire, who, wary
        Of commissions, backs the conspiracy
Theory that the Twin Towers' fated
Fall was powerfully orchestrated.

Like John Kennedy's assassination,
    Will we ever know? The tragedies
That widely befall such a nation
    As ours, someone's likely to keep the keys
        To glitches and muffs. The strategies
Of damage control and spin beat out truth.
Democracies earn their sleuths.

Here's one of those rhetorical questions
    I'm likely to abuse. Poetry is full of them—
The rule being no poet has solutions,
    At least those who make nothing happen:
    "What gave?" ask the critics. The conversion
In '67 at Fisk? Why dull the edge
Of a weapon? Why hand over your badge?

Yusef muses: you suffered in your skin,
    As if *Maud Martha* were a portal
Through the blue-black cold to "Being Gwen-
    Dolyn Brooks." And we, your dark kin, mortals
    Montaged till our hate's a single portrayal:
You carried aloft on the oeuvre of your hearse—
We line the curbs and weep on our hurts.

More distressing than imperial war,
    These lines will land on clogged ears,
Will ne'er jump-start modern delight for
    Reading habits like Top 40 I fear
    Make what's fashionable soon dreary,
E.g., L=A=N=G=U=A=G=E poetry; the darling
Of the runway once, now lacks a farthing's

Worth of mystique: her legs aged, her eyes
    Tapped of all glitz and indifference.
She's the tragic, flash-in-the-pan vamp eyeing
    A café window. Epicureans
    Dining on decadence, eerily Darwinian.
What age granted these lines material good?
Can the epistolary form contain our hoods?

Wyoming

Your own Social Aid & Pleasure
    Club, your benevolence seemed old world,
So many checks bestowed; your signature
    Was scripture spreading the good word:
        "Where there is no gift there is no art," the pearl
Even Wm. Gates finds spiritually enhancing,
Proof every Medici knows, "Giving is good living."

Which reminds me,—no adequate Thank You
    Conveys the perennial debt I owe,
That morning you chose to forgo the choo-
    Choo to Manhattan. Instead, my stereo
    VW played Kravitz's "Flowers for Zoë"
On cruise control as we schlepped up I-95—
The weight of your fate in part kept us alive.

Although too many showings can be a chore,
    You stopped in Philly at the Painted Bride,
Your esteemed Jefferson Lecture tour.
    True to reputation, you inscribed
    Copies of books for the many meek-eyed
Admirers, giving each your full presence.
At midnight, I thought, "Brooks for President."

Everyone knows you rarely took off
    In a flying machine, the railway
Your preferred choice of travel. A chauf-
    Feur, still, is best when one wants by day
    Affable company to chat away

The prior night's tensile stress or to court
A fresh disciple disguised as one's escort.

Jersey, the industrial carcass, one
    Of the great literary states we agreed
Which, of course, begged the question
    About landscape: Does a poet's muse need
    Her own wasteland to succeed?
Then, to each a refinery or a smokestack
Or junkie in the alley with a baseball bat.

I felt less the stranger, something in you
    That carried at once the high dignity
Of your calling (seldom practiced by few)
    As the face of a race, and the sprightly
    Girl still in awe. The world freaks with Foxy.
We've lost the uplift, the decorum and light.
Can you picture Li'l Kim in a Rohan Crite?

I struck up conversation about "Riot"
    Somewhere near Newark International;
John Cabot, condescension not–
    Withstanding, seemed a sacrificial
    Figure, martyr on the altar of racial
Warfare, his plunge beneath the will of the folk
No less woeful hidden by blood & smoke.

To which you replied, "Absolutely not."
    (Seems I pushed the limits of your munificence.)
For you, Cabot was more than a bigot;
    His brand of intolerance? Transcendent,
    Given wings by a rank aestheticism, hence
You could not afford an ounce of empathy
For snobs who rose above humanity.

Still feeling the sting of your rebuttal,
    (More the misread artist's reprimand)
We pulled over. Nice! The Plaza Hotel,
    Central Park South. A black-caped doorman
    Jaunted curbside, opened your door,
"Welcome Back Ms. Brooks." His words allayed fears
You'd be hurt while in my care,

An anxiety brought on by a wide-eyed
    Worship, mark of the afflicted
Would-be author longing to join the tide
    Of shadows thinking. The conflicted
    Liaison H. Bloom sought to depict
Seems flawed; ephebes love their precursors—
It's their words that are the oppressors.

The venetians failed to close. We gave
    Ceilings their only glances and gasped
Like pages at light opening. "How brave,"
    We said, "petals inside bubbles." Grass
    Spread up a door. Auteurs donned masks
Then swapped their names for eternal time.
Books stacked up,—the spine of mankind.

What fevered my wrist was this: you could
    Have amicably thanked me for the ride,
Extending your elbow-length glove, you could
    Have disappeared in that opulent façade,
    Instead you asked if I'd read alongside
That night. I left and bought a pad from Kmart
Then wrote all the poems I knew by heart,

Which numbered two,—one of those, a haiku.
    The evening thickens dense as trees
Except the feel of reading on stage with you.
    Truth be told, I've come to believe such deeds
    Define as much the black tradition and seed
The garden Clarence Major speaks. If it thrives,
Scores bend on hand and knee keeping it alive.

As much I deem firm black poets cultivate
    A knack at verse, without sponsors
Beating drums manuscripts disintegrate.
    Think Wheatley growing silent in a drawer
    Or the world having never read Harper's
Dear John, Dear Coltrane, one you saw to light—
Think Dr. King tom-tomming civil rights.

Ted Joans sat in the audience, hip
    I recall, back from "who-knows-where," a sharp,
Red, bow tie altared a beard which flourished
    Full round his avuncular face. He remarked
    On your role as poetry's matriarch.
Then tossed from a pocket a flower,
"La plus belle Africaine in your honor."

I love that photo I dug up online,
    He and Ginsberg puckering for a smooch,
The way a snapshot creates lineage.
    Love lies in that hectic stillness. What suits
    Joans the Surrealist, desire muted
Bursting in the rivers of our dreams—
There black flowers affix their beam.

Once, Ursula, he and I sought beauties
   At the Philadelphia Museum
& found The Drawings of Joseph Beuys:
   "In Thinking Is Form." Much amused
   By her form, Ted urged her to be his muse
In Paris, as Frida Kahlo's granddaughter.
Ever since, her poems enchant like scripture water.

I smell fresh coffee brewing. My cup's weak.
   These Adirondack chairs seem made
For summer lounging. Kati's likely wreaking
   Havoc on a puzzle. She'll ask for aid,
   But needs next to little. "Author Kincaid.
Seven-letter word beginning with J?"
The eager in-law, I'll chime later "Quai d'Orsay."

Hunting Park

I am weary of light over Herring Cove,
    Setting off the urge to pen an aubade.
Yet, all of us in the parking lot drove
    To catch day break the horizon. Cape Cod's
    A place of wit where each their own God.
I've seen her in every glitter. The terns dive
With such passion. My heart breaks. I am alive.

I have a few minutes which to scribble
    More my paranormal memo.
I drink Tedeschi coffee and nibble
    On a muffin. Outside my window,
    A mess of gulls lurks, expecting me to throw
The day's rations. I thumb and eat every crumb.
Thanks to the Fine Arts Work Center, I have come

With Langston to offer my little know-how
    On tinkering poems. This is our father-
Son time. He's on the verge of twelve. How
    Did he grow up so fast? Today, we'll gather
    A gift and visit Stanley Kunitz after
I've talked at length on a poem's rhetorical
Moves, that is, how to make any stanza groove.

I longed for a bar mitzvah when I turned
    His age, some imminent ritual that marked
My neurotic suffering and sudden concern
    For the grave, having realized I'd embarked,
    With no say in the matter, on a slow walk

Towards that unfathomable future
Which seemed aimless as I was sure

How the journey would decisively end.
    (That's no pun.) My start and stop shared
A dot, so I thought. (Well, you're the maven
      Now on this point.) At twelve, I despaired
        Till I read *Le Mythe de Sisyphe*. Camus aired
My darkest thoughts (and the ghetto luckless
Who often pronounced, *I don't give a fuck*).

I wiped the black rings from round my eyes,
    I was the lead singer next for The Cure,
Sans the mop of foppish hair, then devised
      A plan that would give the journey texture,
      Meaning, what Lowell rather reassuringly
Deemed *a loophole for the soul*. I would
Carve these squares, turn speech to shaped wood.

I would make poems that organized time,
    Frame the inevitable so that its trail
Were made visible, a kind of bullet time.
      Notice, in The Matrix, each breath exhaled,
      Peerless as the last. Stanley's washed-up whale
Helps sculpt the turning of the years,
Puts us close to mysteries of the spheres.

Art as ritual, said again and again,
    Most recently by DJ Spooky,
Who cites the sound collage as transcendent
      Rite building a nation, our esprit
      De corps. Hip-hop's current genius loci
Believes the cut, scratch, and spin
Amends heteroglossia & situates Bakhtin.

Over the year, I've requested of friends to write
    Postcards to Langston on his birthday,
To share notable moments and rites
    Of passage. We lack non-secular ways
    Of insuring their grasp of that crucial phase:
When they should discover their emotional might,
Thus the custom of visiting a revered poet.

May this letter be kind to time, preserve
    The fibers which bind their inspired intent;
May it revere Ts'ai Lun and his superb
    Dream: pounding wood to pulp, but may it
    Also serve as the "thank you" no amount
Of bread, roses, or honorary degrees
Could ever deign or survive under siege.

Convention dictates I invoke a god
    Or two. I'll need them; I tend to be long
Winded. For my purposes, a simple nod
    Would do, one that says, "Keep the song
    Taut and chic." and thus my instrument (all wrong
The avant-garde cheeps), the rime royal,
Grounds to some for complete disavowal,

Those who would revoke my poet card,
    Who would charge me with class ascension,
Who would banish me to the stockyard
    Of single-raced anthologies or mention
    Such asinine folly as, "His attention
To rhyme?—weak shot to procure a public.
It's little wonder this will even publish."

To wit, sounds are political; a line reckoned
    Conservative adhering to meter.
While Liberals stream like chanting wiccans,
    Eco-fems enlarge their massive peters.
    The 'Crats compose by space heaters.
Progressives are equally polysemous.
Independents advance on Uncle Remus.

O, Orpheus, grant the skills to stir
    The dead like Kanye mixing music with fire,
Spitting souls through wires. Let me chauffeur
    The true and living through muck and mire,
    Rescue the underground so they aim higher.
Grant the gift to chisel words like De Beers.
Let them dangle,—verbal gems for their ears.

Erie

I put a premium on rhymes—how could I
    Not living the times of the Supa
Emcees where styles are def, lyrics fly,
    Tight the way our minds move over
    Beats and grooves. Our brain matter's
Amped, mic-checked so we non-stop.
My spirit feels echoes thanks to hip-hop.

I thought to send a note to 2Pac,
    Then wondered if he is there with you.
Rumor has it he's far from dead,—that in fact
    He lives like Assata in Cuba
    Having fled Death Row. His mask consumes us
Still. A rapper shot, a martyr is born.
Sad not the man but an image we mourn:

Party pack tight shots of supersized flesh
    While laughing, sucker-punched to dance,
Each cameo recording resurrects
    Pool-side queries, "How could I just kill a man?"
    An empire croons, toughed-up in a trance.
Imperialism rotates heavy as the world follows
Our nation's mantra: "clothes, bankrolls, and hoes."

Paradise is a checkpoint of virgins
    For which a vest of bombs body-strapped
Blasts shrapnel eyes into martyrdom.
    So they tell us a river of honey maps
    Fluted glasses of desire. On a raft

Float children of Columbine and Palestine,
Bypassing their lives for an ocean of wine.

A cafeteria was all one needed:
    A beat-box firm as the heart. We'd begin
A flow, spitting rhymes that superseded
    Our teacher's verdict: dim-witted children
    Who'll never taste marchand de vin.
Rap's dawning was the earth's reality,
To give a sound to a collective necessity.

Couched in that "We" of the Real always
    Keeping it, that cool defiance, that
Organic email to oppression, hallway
    Leanings and attitudinal grace, that
    Much future you heard, that
Sugar on the Hill ganging up airways,
Those Public Enemy freedom phrases,

Those Boogie Downs and Big Daddy
    Kanes, those Digable Planets & Afro
Names, that Rakim and Mr. Eric B
    Or Disposable Heroes of Hiphoprisy,
    That Salt-N-Pepa & Roxanne Roxanne,
West coast Coolio and fisted X-Clans,
Those Questing Tribes spitting Concertos

Of the Desperadoes, but the Boom Bap's done
    Gone Jiggy, and every other word is Ho
Or Niggy. Nicca: still all the same, one
    Frame of the nation that spells hun-
    Ger, like a straw to the brain, video poison
Normalizes the game, our children pointing guns.
We need life like the Fugees need Lauren.

Lest you're worried, we've yet to extinguish
    The human breath; other forms of life
Are game. Our current president's wish?
    To drill Alaska's natural wildlife
    For oil. Thirty-six species of mammal-life,
One hundred types of birds, polar bears,
Made extinct to fuel his earnings per share.

If only we could unravel how to expunge
    Dollars from the democratic process.
Forbes's list sops up elections like sponges.
    Superman no longer beats his chest;
    He merely licks his pen then writes a check.
"Us versus them" is what Nietzsche tallied.
Campaign dinners are hyped pep rallies.

Too much democracy is a leaning tower,
    Claim wardens of the two-party regime.
Behind my eyes, sun-lit rain showers,
    A flickering hologram, The Supremes
    Singing "I Hear a Symphony," a stream
Of soft petals drizzling what the country means
To me, an arching tower of rainbow beams.

Where you're at, CNN likely reports:
    Who last booted from empyreal
Heights; what indolent angels fell short
    The good-deeds quota; who's left to heal;
    What new arrivals have seen Ezekiel's
Wheel. I've set the task of bringing up to date
All the news down here; the current state

Of poetry, what's in and what's out, sports,
> Fad diets and more. A prophesy: some-
Day we'll dine on info chips in support
> Of ruling elites. Instead of spilling crumbs
> Over The New York Times, thumbing
Through say, trade policies, we'll reach consent
By having numbed the discontents—

Instant news granola light beamed via
> Satellite in the mouth: coverage
Of the environment; ProteinPlus for a
> Company man; a square of shredded "yeas"
> For the health-wise, middle-aged
Woman. No youthful rage, no point of view,
No alt. perspective, no making it new.

Tourists have arrived and assumed their place
> On the sands. Each pitched umbrella
Takes us nearer to southern France. The pace
> Of this letter is a little, I know, slow. Fela's
> Playing on the local radio. I'll leaf
These pages with greater speed. I'm off. You've time.
I'll clap our lives as one with a later rhyme.

Cecil B. Moore

Gwen, I am glad you're not living at this hour,
    For we are like the kid pushed in a yard
Who pushes back, then finding his power,
    Becomes the bully with no regard
    For what hates he sows. How soon our scars
Fade. The light of an empire ages. Daily seas
Rumble below repeating man's history.

September triggered a rash
    Of abuses, all around. I am concerned
For Langston's future. We are not rich
    Enough to avoid conscription. He'll earn
    His stripes, I hope, by not harming
Other parents' children, but performing acts
Of diplomacy, which today smack

Of the dress rehearsal before the attack.
    How would you have responded? Images
Of men and women beheaded or stacked
    Before a camera, the mental war waged
    In our name? Who foretold the carnage?
Or the beast beneath our skin? how we proclaim
Civility, then digitize the cave whence we came?

Our psyche takes the beating, six hooded
    Iraqis lurk behind us in our dreams.
When the axe swings, we awaken, doomed
    To not hear the Sanskrit above our screams.
    My grandfather came on the scene the same

Year as you. Stunning to think of the horrors
Of the century in his head. In a corner,

The child in him crouches as the room darkens.
    He was born to a world at war & expects
To die a night of bombs evening the score. When
    I fire up my laptop & cam, he shirks
    & cannot take more of the world at work,
Enough electric spanking he seems to say,
Nor believes men on the moon, to this day.

Question: How much headway can we take?
    Are we advancing faster than our blood
Courses? Much we've already taken
    At a lightning pace, over-flooding
    Perhaps what our brains can endure. You'd
Giggle at the breakthroughs of the past decade,
For one, robots disarming bombs in caves.

The wireless world we live permits instant
    Admission. The Internet shrinks the globe.
We've hotspots to our bank accounts,
    The Hague, stores, our homes. I can disrobe
    On a beach and never cease the work mode,
Like registering students for my classes,
Or answering emails from the lads & lasses.

We've developed at last alternative
    Ways to move our cars. Hybrid engines
Free us all the more from excessive
    Costs at the pump. In our fin
    De siècle despair of OPEC's siphoning
Of American pockets, I predict, once
We're through altogether with oil, the only

Vehicles left to fuel will be machines
    Of war, our children sure to become
Lowell's Ghosts orbiting forever on a big screen,
    A reality show we will likely sell
    To the public as a means of swelling
National pride,—in our time, a hollow value,
The gist zapped from the red, white, and blue.

Of TVs, we hunger for bigger screens, better
    Sounds. XM & Sirius broaden
The waves with satellites and crystal-clear
    Tunes or the news. The man in Tiananmen
    Square and I can synchronize more than
Our thirst for democracy. We can get our fill
On Dylan, Coldplay, and Cypress Hill.

Kids no longer devour dots. Gaming videos
    Turn them to fighters who hunt bad guys.
Fully armed imaginary worlds like Halo
    Insure no one different catches the prize.
    In Grand Theft Auto, they've even devised
Squalid streets that let you explore the thug
Within: soccer moms jacking rides for drugs.

Computer chips are smaller than fingerprints.
    We've acronyms for it all: with GPS
You never guess where you're going. With Sprint
    Phones just about anyone can be a spy.
    Every cell is a cam, and every cam an eye.
Picture the universe through a single bubble,
Planets billions of years away through the Hubble.

An unmanned spacecraft landed on Mars.
    iPods will never leave you without a song.
My students walk the quad like Martians.
    Biotech firms go cloning along.
    Stem cells can remake our bones strong.
We are mapping the human genome;
We'll soon design kids to match our homes.

I looked you up this morning. Eighty-one
    Thousand results with audio links,
Biographies, profiles, and pics, your life summed
    & presented to the tyro in a blink.
    Substitute the Cartesian logic, I think
To "I Google, therefore I am," and you've
Uncovered our zeitgeist, the groove

Of an era, our mark on earth measured
    In binary codes, not by deeds, which total
Many for you. So many claim your sway, treasure
    Your artful phrasings and praise, fall under
    Your spell like electricity to thunder.
I, like them, value you above all else,
Indispensable poet of the public's health.

I begin this stop all wrong: you should be
    Living at this hour. We need your bolts
& resounding poems like we need Sweet Honey
    In the Rock's sacred songs, a revolt
    Against plain figurings, new and bold
Metaphors to help us keep people always
In vision, to fight the corporate bug away.

Spring Garden

When you have forgotten (to bring into
    Play that fragrant morsel of rhetoric,
Crisp as autumnal air), when you
    Have forgotten, say, sunlit corners, brick
    Full of skyline, row homes, smokestacks,
Billboards, littered rooftops & wondered
What bread wrappers reflect of our hunger,

When you have forgotten wide-brimmed hats,
    Sunday back-seat leather rides & church,
The door lock like a silver cane, the broad backs
    Swaying or the great moan deep churning,
    & the shimmer flick of flat sticks, the lurch
Forward, skip, hands up Ailey-esque drop,
When you have forgotten the meaningful bop,

Hustlers and their care-what-may, blasé
    Ballet and flight, when you have forgotten
Scruffy yards, miniature escapes, the way
    Laundry lines strung up sag like shortened
    Smiles, when you have forgotten the Fish Man
Barking his catch in inches up the street,
"I've got porgies. I've got trout. Feeesh

Man," or his scoop and chain scale,
    His belief in shad and amberjack; when
You have forgotten Ajax and tin pails,
    Blue crystals frothing on marble front
    Steps Saturday mornings, or the garden

Of old men playing checkers, the curbs
Whitewashed like two lines out to the burbs,

Or the hopscotch squares painted new
    In the street, the pitter-patter of feet
Landing on rhymes. "How do you
    Like the weather, girls? All in together girls,
    January, February, March, April . . ."
The jump ropes' portentous looming,
Their great, aching love blooming.

When you have forgotten packs of grape-
    Flavored Now and Laters, the squares
Of sugar flattening on the tongue, the elation
    You felt reaching into the corner-store jar,
    Grasping a handful of Blow Pops, candy bars
With names you didn't recognize but came
To learn. All the turf battles. All the war games.

When you have forgotten popsicle stick
    Races along the curb and hydrant fights,
Then, retrieve this letter from your stack
    I've sent by clairvoyant post & read by light.
    For it brought me as much longing and delight.
This week's Father's Day; I've a long ride to Philly.
I'll give this to Gramps, then head to Black Lily.

FROM
Holding Company
(2010)

Picket Monsters

For I was born, too, in the stunted winter of History.
For I, too, desired the Lion's mouth split
& the world that is not ours, and the wounded children
set free to their turnstiles of wonder. I, too, have
blinked speechless at the valleys of corpses, wished
Scriabin's "Black Mass" in the Executioner's ear,
Ellington in the Interrogation Room.
I now seek gardens where bodies have their will,
where the self is a compass point given to the lost.
Let me call your name; the ground here is soft & broken.

Creationism

I gave the bathtub purity and honor, and the sky
noctilucent clouds, and the kingfisher his implacable
devotees. I gave salt & pepper the table, and the fist
its wish for bloom, and the net, knotholes of emptiness.
I gave the loaf its slope of integrity, the countertop
belief in the horizon, and mud its defeated boots.
I gave morning triumphant songs which consume my pen,
and death its grief, which is like a midsummer thunderclap.
But I did not give her my tomblike woe though it trembled
from my white bones and shook the walls of our home.

Going to Meet the Man

As if one day, a grand gesture of the mind, an expired
subscription to silence, a decision raw as a concert
of habaneros on the lips, a renewal to decency like a trash
can smashing a storefront or shattering the glass face
of a time clock: where once a man forced to the ground,
a woman spread-eagled against a wall, where a blast into
the back of an unarmed teen: finally, a decisive spark,
the engine of action, a civilian standoff: on one side,
a barricade of shields, helmets, batons, and pepper spray:
on the other, a cocktail of fire, all that is just and good.

Mondes en Collision

To the question of history's tectonic drift,
Immanuel Velikovsky removed his glasses & pinched
his temples before a silent throng at the Royal
Hypnagogic Society in Edmonton. Through a window,
coppiced trees blurred. An orange-headed thrush
fleetingly invaded his sight. Someone coughed.
Despair fell into despair, building its music. The abrupt clash
of meaning was like the laughter of running children.
He saw the microphone's convexed portals as one
of many recognizable texts out of our celestial holes.

Migration

That summer, municipality was on everyone's lips,
even the earth eaters who put the pastor in pastoral.
Truth is my zeal for chicory waned, and my chest was damp.
I shivered by a flagpole, knowing betrayal
was coming my way. Just the same, I believed like a guitar string
believes in distance and addressed each bright star *Lord
of My Feet*. A country of overnight deputies, everyone had a knot
to endeavor. I read oaks and poplars for signs: charred branches,
tobacco leaves strung up to die, swamp soil in my soul. Ever trace
the outline of a phantom mob, even if you were late arriving?

After Riefenstahl

The screen's fabrications remain. A film
shot never fails, sailing through the century
like a black V at the hour of moaning.
I premiere these pontifical birds: villagers march
and raise their arms, Marschlieder. Thus I am
your sweet messenger glittering more than first stars,
a harvest of light concealing your nicks and little deaths.
My comrade, my camera, my power, my fury,
my triumph, my will: do you not also,
my love, flicker in a cathedral of terror?

Roof of the World

I live on the roof of the world among the aerial
simulacra of Things, among the faded: old tennis shoes,
vanished baseballs, heartbreak gritted with dirt. My mind
flickers like lightning in a cloud. I'm networked
beholding electric wires and church spires.
I lean forward and peer at the suffering below—
Sartre said: man is condemned to be free.
I believe in the dead who claim to believe in me—
says, too, the missing and forgotten. Day darkens
on. I hear our prayers rising. I sing to you, now.

Greek Revival

Of that unhurried blink of eyelids I glimpsed, all pixilated
and grains, belonging to a woman dying, on screen
her life winding down, yet one last cinematic glance
in the prime like a loose smile filling the frame
over a shoulder, I say so much lateral interpolations
fasten us to that sequence of flowers as sped-up funerals. I thought
this, stepping up in the Garden District to a streetcar.
The avenue has rituals: the curved horizon of Southern
mansions, and the gripping anguish of oak branches
reaching through half-opened windows like desperate fingers.

Said the Translator

Plato would be easier, said the translator, and thus began
the factory tour. One had to understand the language
of AstroTurf dotted with cannons or the nonalcoholic joy
subway-watching women two-finger designer eyewear
firmly up the bridge, all that rollicking uncertainty
like a root beer. Who cares about splitting hairs,
when what's at stake is merely the history of robes?
The clock read 12:13, exactly when no seven were alike,
yet, give him a pencil and the knotholes of other mouths
make a soft hollow noise. All he knows is what he thinks.

Jane Says

I only know they want me, prone to stupefaction
and the ambivalence of men. The house is sleeping,
but she's flipping through American Spirits,
the canned laughter of heroin nights. Her oneiric
fade: prairie grass bending away, barnyard decay,
red-checkered tableware, summer running liquid
air, languorous lift of an American flag, her grandparents
waving, her worn duffle bag, the Irish setter
spiraling in circles. A patrol car paints more tattoos,
and out of silence, they move, too, like green vines.

Lost Lake

A soggy brightness at the northernmost ridge
of the Tahkenitch, even nearing dusk and not
a Domino's for miles. I said holy at a coniferous wall
of western hemlock overhead and red cedar
which rose up from the foot of that coastal creek
bearing its image and all around. I had not known
I'd come as a witness. The great Pacific rolled in
news from distant shores beyond a stretch of dune
trails behind us. White-winged gulls shrieked
and flapped at our misery frothing in waves.

I Had the Craziest Dream

Never on Sunday, she said and brandished
an oval locket of hairs from each
of her lovers. I looked over my shoulders.
We sat munching on puffs of dried hydrangea
that, no surprise, tasted of cotton candy.
Far off on the sea, on a floating bench,
my mother excitedly talked up the president.
I questioned his killing clothes, and knew it all perishable
at any moment. The pictures hung themselves
along our coastline. *Best,* she said, *to hammer in the morning.*

Life during Wartime

But the daydream collapses and time returns us
to corners where young boys expire
like comets at the suburbs of your thalamus.
Gunshots weaken the houses; hope vanishes
like old cellphones. Blood darkens a stoop;
the mouth is disagreeable. But then, one afternoon,
a sunshower baptizes shadows on a street. The steaming
scent of wet sidewalks swells your insides
and somewhere not far from here a young girl grabs
the hand of a boy and runs over the rubble.

Dynagroove

Our social clock had gone berserk but those
groovy Eames and collectible lamps licensed
us to practice a kind of savage civility. Our vice
wasn't noble or the avalanche of cocktails
with serene names suggestive of spy movies
or the imprudent idea of going further in snow.
We secretly wished for living rooms with such large
cushions. We might have survived it all, especially
the piñata beatings of effigies in foreign deserts we had
no idea existed. Even the bongos promised Heaven.

New Sphere of Influence

This is the year I'll contemplate the fire-fangled sky
over the isle of Pag, authored by my lover's eyes.
A crimson rambler uncurls its petals, and I am whistling
a dusty concerto, *Hope with Roadside Wildflowers*.
I want to unfurl in the sodden fields of her daydreams.
Who wants immortality if she must die?
Once I thought stars were everlasting, only dying
behind a cerulean curtain, cloudy rains at dawn.
My lover's lips are twin geniuses. I've trashed the movie stubs
of my past. I've front row seats to her mumbling sleep.

Towers

I could give your palace more glass shine,
facing eastward every year without knowing.
And no, it's not convincing waking in fog and rain,
steel and stone soaring above the living. After many
springs, streets accrue their grief, and the people
are nameless. I broadcast my hunger,
heartwood beneath skin radiant as coronas—
what's there: son of tenderness, son of disasters.
When the lonely swirl nights, I run toward them,
a concentric eyewall, my indestructible hunger.

Anthrodrome

She was light as a shadow. I wanted
to know her better than the rest
before me. I promised her neither miracles
or hallucinations and mixtaped all
my ecstasies starting first with Sembène.
Out of my mouth came the wind
of my birth. Out of my hands poured unteachable
rain. Seeing nothing but inappropriate sentinels,
products of major antagonisms from a far-off century,
we said Good-bye to our once born emptiness.

Heaven Goes Online

When the sidewalk's eyes were weeping
when snowflakes burst from the pillows
as the mayor talked from the bottlecaps of his ears
& the old women dusted off their beauty marks
when the graffiti artist's hand became a saffron scarf
when the breeze flashed its grilled teeth
& the sun torched the forest to a moon
when sad Amelia pierced the clouds in her veins
when my lips gathered at the beaches of your lips
& my tongue at the on-ramp of your spine

Manna

As if every evening your body is a smile
mingling with the sea or the sky's last song
over the cenotaph of violets wilting in Eastham.
On the day of the crime, the afternoon was empty.
We were footnotes on the beach and came back the color
of pancakes. I was giving the Rosicrucians another chance,
knowing how hunger prevails long after we've turned
our backs on cruelty toward Faulkner and Seneca.
My gratitude was fragile, for I was kissing the thorns.
"To sea! To sea!" shouted the marvelous girls, "To sea!"

The Door I Open

The door I open to who I am is not a garage
of reminisces or a book with you
as an elastic notion represented in between
stanzas, thus a hall of Mona Lisas. The door
I open is a self-song furnishing the mind's
mansion. I observe no rules and ruin the hours.
Plato knew the poem as a sword moonlighting
as a mirror which correctly angled caught a surfeit
of light and threatened to blind the Republic—
our rotoscopic freedom at the foothills.

Designer Kisses

I'm glum about your sportive flesh in the empire of blab,
and the latest guy running his trendy tongue like a
tantalizing surge over your molars, how droll. Love by a graveyard is
redundant, but the skin is an obstacle course like Miami where we are
inescapably consigned: tourists keeping the views new.
What as yet we desire, our own fonts of adoration. By
morning, we're laid out like liquid timepieces, each other's exercise
in perpetual enchantment, for there is that beach in us that is
untranslatable; footprints abound. I understand: you're at a clothes
    rack at Saks
lifting a white linen blouse at tear's edge wondering.

Fever

Had I possessed the poise to kick
aside my faraway thirst for mornings or the wide
solo in a listening glass emptied of speech, had I
possessed the incorruptible sermons
of windowpanes, or danced a little more in the lush
inscriptions of your gaze—I, who believe in the fauna
of dreams, in the hand that tunes a guitar, in the will
of pages, might have journeyed to you
like ash and abandoned all my fires, and named the epic
light over your shoulders and seized your tumbledown.

Lorca in Eden

Squat by a roadside near Eden, prairie flowers,
barnyard decay, spray of stars bulleting above,
I summon the great poet & pitch my loneliness
across his lake, my chest exploding like milkweed,
nothing more than a stripped hull of seed fluff:
un paisaje prodigioso, pero de una melancolía
infinita . . . No cesa de llover. This moonlight is gruesome,
so many hearts teased to a nakedness then bleached,
frayed, deflated, flapping like scarves in nightwinds—
their radiant mangling all over this meadow of silk.

On the Manner of Addressing Shadows

that were not ours though we understood their lives,
their sudden advent, daylight painting our façades
when we turned onto Broad Street, oncoming traffic
of strangers, their sudden jolt upright and undulation
should any delivery truck maneuver across their somber torsos
spilling off the curb, even then, still their dark
addiction to our soles. Gloomy sidekicks,
you are cemetery dirt cast unto a cloud that falls
into a city of inevitable demise. You make lords of us,
though we understand your need to detach & walk away.

Treat the Flame

As if the whole inferno. It's a melodrama
for any gambler embroidered with bells
on her vest who knows if you over-attention
your syntax, every surface is fustian at best.
The sound played is of many foghorns.
All the time I had been dreaming of lost prisms,
the hand's plumage and drift. This is one reason
I think perhaps I drowned in so many puddles
posing as rivers, the eloquence of mirrors.
You are right to detest your inner pyro.

Periplum

The notion that the land gave us flying
you said, or, conceivably, flying made us
aware of the notion of land was your most recent
attempt to strike a lasting chord. Of course,
this exposed our admiration for the hard-hatted surveyor
wide-eyeing a dumpy level. There is in me someone
who would rather fall out a window, Buster Keaton–like,
and come up important like a tripod. Gurdjieff nearly
cried for collaboration. We both pointed to his
eminently readable mustache: graspable yet airborne.

Leave It All Up to Me

All we want is to succumb to a single kiss
that will contain us like a marathon
with no finish line, and if so, that we land
like newspapers before sunrise, halcyon
mornings like blue martinis. I am learning
the steps to a foreign song: her mind
was torpedo, and her body was storm,
a kind of Wow. All we want is a metropolis
of Sundays, an empire of hand-holding
and park benches. She says, "Leave it all up to me."

Forecast

Whichever way our shoulders move, there's joy.
Make a soft hollow noise. We've our own hourglass
and no one else to blame. I thought of our lives,
caressing ruins through half-opened windows.
I hear our prayers rising. I sing to you, now,
like scented candles, your ferocious wolf.
I no longer want this weather on my breath
or the many recognizable texts of our celestial holes.
A ceiling fan turns above. The arson is in us.
This is the year I'll contemplate the fire-fangled sky.

FROM
Roll Deep
(2015)

Reverse Voyage

My midway journey, my emancipated eyes
like runaways, exposed, and the row homes stacked
again, colorless drab LEGO blocks. I come
back to unlit alleys, avenues in sheaths of grit
and utility wires like veins stitched to power supplies
buzzing above a different kind of hum.
Just when my seeing was rectifying into
something faultless, extraordinary as a cat's refuge
beneath a parked car, I'm brought back to
the silence, oblique, hidden deep inside
the ventricle caves of my body's chambers,
to nail salons, check cashing stores, pawnshops.
How characteristic of them to greet me though,
the old folk, in such a way: magisterial.
The corner store with its faded graffiti lines,
finally whitewashed, nearly expunged,
doubtless like its author save for his palimpsest,
and yet, behind a first-floor window, a young boy bends
over an old encyclopedia, a remarkable script,
a genuine compendium that shows his people's Africa
like a sculpted mask for tourists in an open market
which he slowly turns contemplating skin, the color
of almonds, pyramids, revolutions, and other such beauties.
Human strength never before seen kept those
mystical relations alive until they touched themselves
again, revived songs albeit injured, but no less rich.
Even here, all's remixed. In Fairmount Park,
a posse plays the same din with fresher strains
of freedom, what never passes. That is the message,
always, of its august lines, a rangy dignity,
the lesson, too, of what one refuses to never forget
about this place: a grandmother, Mrs. Pearl, a domestic,

thirty years boarding SEPTA early mornings.
I think of her, clutching a tan purse, statelier than these lines.
So oblivion vacates memory—these connecting
columns of bricks, and wires, and me, its last deportee
which the blood sings no matter snowcaps,
no matter mountainous ranges and glittering lakes
like flashing daggers, no matter allegory of hoarfrost,
no matter tractor parades and morning
finches and bluejays that skitter my sight in a valley
far away from city pigeons who hop and settle off electric
wires near street gutters to peck heads at one crumb
or another, where local inhabitants, too, study skies
with a certainty affixed to rooftops and flashing
underbelly green & red lights going elsewhere or nowhere.
The city's skyscrapers tower: a retired bricklayer
and his wife, the old folk, locked in a grid of streets and their
still-standing three-story on a strip of mostly weed-laden lots,
like a tore-up mouth, where their minds recall,
for sixty years, just where to lay a hand on a railing
& then the stairs that not long ago led up to you or me.
The white marbled steps and boarded-up doorways
and basement windows spilling out debris and rusted springs,
say *Return to us. You've become all there is
to become*: the mocking, blissful smile of an addict
who's half here, nods off on a stoop in a miniskirt,
understanding too well the perpetual voyage then suddenly
jolts up to greet cars sparkling like sin, slowing to a stop
while her daughter upstairs puts both hands under her chin,
amused for years, watching a flickering stream of endless images.
And always I call a taxi or pack my rental
and inaudibly say *no*, recalling afternoons
my eyes rarely veered from a book,
even while walking one day from middle school
when a boy lunged a fist in my stomach

like a question mark. I was already awake,
a surfeit of ambition struck: to roam
like decomposing clouds rolling deep,
re-forming constantly and away, above
toughened streets, above sunlit ruins
and scattering mounds. My eyes went
elsewhere or nowhere, open and determined.

Urban Renewal

XXI. Greece

The Cyclades Blues Suite / i.

On the *Aegean Speed Line*, hightailing a fast ferry
away from Perseus's birthplace, away from those beaches
with names like *Ganema, Sykamia, Megalo Livadi*,
whose scythe-like coves left us speechless
and shockingly bold as we unpeeled our bathing suits
like human wrappers, letting pebbly sand stick
to our backs, while the sun conducted its trade routes.
We ask: *Why are we departing again?* Homesick
we are not, though we did wish our three sons
here, so as to astonish that *we* were the better
parents, and surely I cursed the island for its urchins
who fired missiles when my hand sought treasures
near their spiky orbs. I understand now why
children and the dead are abandoned: heaven is a cult
of the irrational. In my glazed-over eyes, your body
found an ally; I rubbed sunscreen until the tumult
in our lives cured right on the spot. Now on deck,
an illness returns. Paradise dwindles to a speck.

ii.

Never get used to this: the morning slow prayer of palm
leaves, feisty light caressing the cubed
halls on the hills in the Chora, the mewling psalms
of homeless cats, surf roiling its evaporating tubes;
salute the snails climbing in clusters like Salgado's miners
up the stalk of some flower, since what you grieve is not
the sublime change of seasons, but the major
hurts you caused in loving too many women. That hot
orb dazzles the heart to a spectacle but you've one more
chance to focus like the Greek sparrow balanced
on the precipice of a roof, nest matter in his mouth
looking for a moment to the shore, then like a lance
taking flight to build a home. Never get used to this:
yucca leaves lifting like a chorus of arms,
the garnishing blue of the Aegean Sea splitting
your eyes into a million sparkling charms.

iii.

Every island is filled with loneliness, even Serifos,
where a donkey's eye is a suffering despondent,
where Father Makarious makes the sign of the cross
as waves arrive like faithful correspondents
and tamarisk trees tender shade like floating coins
and a fisherman slaps his octopus again and again
on a stone by the bay of Livadi at dawn,
and the dazzling nipples of Americans redden
to rusted dials, sharing one sun, where one may take
such signs as nature's camaraderie, except that waitress
who cuts her listless eyes so deep she stakes
you to that label *tourist*, as though excess were the body's
supply at every given place, especially at night
when studded lights mend the horizon where cars zigzag
terraced mountains, and what's heard are voices blown
for thousands of years over villas beyond sagebrush
that bears your grief so familiar you weep.

XXII. Spain

La Barraca Blues Suite / i.

for Mark Strand

Beneath canopies of green, unionists marched doggedly
outside *The Embassy*. Their din was no match
for light lancing through leaves of madrone trees
lining the Paseo then flashing off glossy black *Maybachs*
skidding round a plaza like a monarch fleeing the paparazzi.
Your voice skipped and paused like a pencil.
Layers of morning pastries flaked gingerly
then fell, soft as vowels, on a china plate. One learns
to cherish the wizened reserve of old world manners,
two blotched hands making wings of a daily paper
beside us between sips of café con leche, a demeanor
in short gentle as grand edifices along this boulevard.
Yet *Guernica* is down the street, and some windshields
wear a sinister face, sometimes two. Think Goya. Just south
of here, on the lower slopes of the Sierras, fields
of olive groves braid the land like a Moorish head, but
those sultans were kicked out long ago. In the lobby
of the *Hotel Urban*, I wait for a cab, my obedient rolling bag
like a pet beside me. I have loved again another city
but Madrid is yours: her caped *olé*'s, her bullish flag,
her glass pavilions and outdoor tables like a festival
of unbroken laughter, our dark harbors, finding level.

ii.
Salobreña

That stretch of mountains features white windmill
blades whose slow turns are rifles aiming, for I cannot
help but think of Lorca's killing between here and the
village Alfacar, and the firing squad's gun pops are that flamencan
dancer's heel stomps. I bring back, too, her brisk hand claps
and the cantor's Andalusian moans like dried sticks,
or bones crumbling in his throat. Only souvenir shops
and steep winding streets accrete in this region's stacked
brochures. Her dress spills across the restaurant's floor
like a red shadow, darker than billboards of black bulls
high above roadways, motionless but seeming to gallop
like Franco's brigades. All seeing is an act of war.
Tanks and artillery or Spanish castles and mosques?
I choose to lose, and beneath a watercolorist's sky
study Didi's splendor, nude against the unruffled backdrop
of the Alboran Sea whose waves match my sighs
and bomb this beach, launching sprays of white duds.

iii.
Córdoba, Mezquita

Even if he'd pulled over to study Andalusia's road signs,
after one thousand and one nights, he still could
not make out its calligraphic script, its vertical lines,
its dots, marks like smoke stilled from incense, its curled
sand-soft Arabic, but this city's voice has coffins
and carnations, and its hoarse singing shoots through him
like twelve bars of earthen road that lengthens
into a labyrinth of knowing blood beneath black skin.
More echoes: the Alhambra sent him back to the seraglio
of his youth where a Moorish guard stood in a museum,
unfazed by a harem's rising laughter behind palace doors.
Here are pillars and banded arches to once again
imagine the body passing through like a key into infinity.
Was this the answer to his ghetto past? But why travel
so far? Since a child, even in sleep, he voyaged and broke free,
tossing dice in dreams, once below deck on a caravel
next to grains of paradise. He's collecting a thousand faces.
He's moving beneath eyelids, turning time into flesh.
Don't judge him. The courtyard's orange trees where once
he washed like a morisco are teaching his tongue the craft.

XXIII. Brazil

Berimbau

You, bow-shaped recipe of opulent whines
on steel wire, who keeps the buzz on an acrobat's spine,
or in a circle, open-aired against the city's noise, or
silent in a studio—at night especially—before
a bustling round of capoeiristas' flying kicks, strike
me a pageant of notes and tell how the snake
wriggles free its skin, how bones laid at a door
curse him who crosses a sill, how in Congo Square
on Sundays, African dances kept six hundred slaves alive,
how war defines a century, how the last goodbye
is often a surprise, how the silver bars of a ladder
means someone needs setting free, or sadder
still, how we must always answer *Who are we?*: that is,
we're set upon by gourd & stone; you're the crisis
I hear when I bend to kiss my son, or when,
at a bar standing, see my brown face in a glass of rum.

XXIV. Kenya

The Dadaab Suite / i.

The UN Somali driver speeds by a small herd
of white cattle prodded along by a desert farmer.
Rust-colored dust in its wake clouds barbed-wire
suburbs of white tents and makeshift shelters
of twigs and branches breeding the plateau faster
than malarial flies. I have come to Dadaab like an actor
on a press release, unprepared for the drained faces
of famine-fleeing refugees, my craft's glamour
dimmed by hundreds of infant graves, children
whose lolling heads' final drop landed on their mothers'
backs like soft stones. What beauty can I spell in
this swelter of dust? Ridged like that farmer's
goats, the ribs of others protrude and make a mockery
of my pen. Where is my empathy? The drought
is in my heart as well as on their skins. Yesterday, I walked
the Maasai Mara and saw how nature bears out
its designs: hyenas drew near for the attack; seconds
later, the sound of crushing bones racked my ears;
a battalion of lions gorged on a half-eaten gazelle.
Two nonchalant giraffes glided by like war profiteers.

viii.

In the placid lean of an arid summer, in the lingering
snarl of pit latrines, the sharp barbs of the acacia
thorn tree, in the opaque eyes of the girl fingering
frenziedly her arm's badge of skin suffering cholera,
unearth a feeling for a people who are not your own,
in the sinister look of the man beneath a koofiyad
(he is not al-Shabaab), in the boy selling refurbished phones
in the market, wary of your presence, your queries, the aloof
gaze of women behind hijabs who flee
your camera's barrel, who swiftly turn and cover,
in this land devoid of vegetation like a dried sea
that stretches to their war-torn country scarred over
like a child soldier's back. The camps swell in singeing heat,
hot as empty air of eyeless politicians who have no stake
in other clans. Embrace the father who chews khat,
the girl who sells her limbs for all her body can take.
Think of the rootless, the dispersed, when you slide
into the porcelain glove of your tub like an emperor,
call back the Horn of Africa. Close the divide.
For fear of despair's reprisal, pray they love in return.

XXV. Italy

The Augustan Suite / i.

for Derek Walcott

The blessed will not care what angle they are regarded from.

> W. H. *Auden*

Cobbled streets have the burnished look of stone skulls
sinking like a necropolis of Ugolinos from centuries
of bewildered tourists stumped in the Eternal City, mulling
over which way to turn. Every ruin begets a selfie
like a Hollywood set directed to life then ditched
with each phone's shutter click. Past the bronzed
façade of the Colosseum, ominous as a chipped gold tooth,
other crowds follow like apostles the voice of a guide, yawning
and carrying her flag aloft like a cross. Even here I look for
a history of myself. In the *Musei Vaticani*, I zoom close
to Art's record: frescoes, sculptures, altarpieces, and war
with pilgrims for the best shot, studying the prose
of a guidebook to explain Exekias's amphora,
the slave boy delivering clothes to a nude Pollux,
or why every Christ child craves the adoration of a
black Magus: *shades frozen in a single hole.*
The crumbling stone beneath our feet speaks to us;
even Rome's dust possesses something of human
grandeur, the elegance of decay. I envy the triumph
that certain paintings give back my face, but *Romanus
Pontifex* almost sealed my fate. I have more hills to climb.
From every gift shop, Papa waves at his blessed lambs.

ii.
The Great Beauty

One evening someone will dream of Tuscany and see us
walking along a narrow country road past Relais
San Bruno, plum-littered, beside the north-facing slopes
of vines like formations of green soldiers on their way
to nowhere, a stray dog trotting ahead like Hecuba
who halts and impatiently looks back, checking
our progress to San Biagio. If dreams are rumors,
we are sliding into the light of prayer, practicing
soliloquies of silence in our first year of marriage,
our astonishment punctuated by those cypresses
whose exclamations put a point to blessings. Offstage,
if that sleeper should change pose, and half undress
herself of sheets, let her shift not break cataclysmic
and lose sight of the stone-bright travertine walls,
nor the hills rolling soft as her body, these ancient brick
farmhouses, nor morning's rustic tinkling call
of sheep bells, the honeyed fortress of this city whose blush
of red poppies in fields below collapses some tourist,
our dreamer, into the arms of her husband, crushed
by the view from Montepulciano, nor the way she holds his
hand against her chest lost in a pasture of tiny dwellings
whose faith repeats in campaniles that reach her deepest wells.

iii.

We must be rooted in the absence of place.
Simone Weil

That window at the Grand Hotel Palazzo in Livorno
framed the Tyrrhenian Sea like a white-bordered postcard
he placed gently on an imaginary wire rack below
other views accruing whose postmarks
he'd yet to stamp, so they swiveled in his mind
involuntarily and slowed with a squeak: perched angels
standing guard on the bridge of Sant'Angelo, the crenelated line
of cliffs above some coast, a shop owner waving farewell,
a series of roundabouts whose circles he never
completed, the half-erect heads of sunflowers like a cavalry
in training, all clichés of travel, even the waterfront *terrazza*
with its checkerboard squares. But not her pillowed beauty
still sunk in sleep, a soft coating of night sweat on her face,
her neck lengthening into a Modigliani. The arrowing flashes
of fallen stars he prayed upon were superfluous; their places
changed, but she, she would remain like the horizon whose light
increased, flooding their rented room. Dawn arrived, the shrieking
seagulls circled into view, next, a ferry, launched to fulfill its routes.
Flip this over, a scene scrawled in lines clear as Greek, stealthily
composed then slipped under his door like a hotel receipt.

On Disappearing

I have not disappeared.
The boulevard is full of my steps. The sky is
full of my thinking. An archbishop
prays for my soul, even though
we met only once, and even then, he was
busy waving at a congregation.

The ticking clocks in Vermont sway
back and forth as though sweeping
up my eyes and my tattoos and my metaphors,
and what comes up are the great paragraphs
of dust, which also carry motes
of my existence. I have not disappeared.
My wife quivers inside a kiss.
My pulse was given to her many times,

in many countries. The chunks of bread we dip
in olive oil are communion with our ancestors,
who also have not disappeared. Their delicate songs
I wear on my eyelids. Their smiles have
given me freedom, which is a crater
I keep falling in. When I bite into the two halves
of an orange whose cross-section resembles my lungs,

a delta of juices burst down my chin, and like magic,
makes me appear to those who think I've
disappeared. It's too bad war makes people
disappear like chess pieces, and that prisons
turn prisoners into movie endings. When I fade
into the mountains on a forest trail,
I still have not disappeared, even though its green façade
turns my arms and legs into branches of oak.

It is then I belong to a southerly wind,
which by now you have mistaken as me nodding back
and forth like a Hasid in prayer or a mother who has just
lost her son to gunfire in Detroit. I have not disappeared.

In my children, I see my bulging face
pressing further into the mysteries.

In a library in Tucson, on a plane above
Buenos Aires, on a field where nearby burns
a controlled fire, I am held by a professor,
a general, and a photographer.
One burns a finely wrapped cigar, then sniffs
the scented pages of my books, scouring
for the bitter smell of control.
I hold him in my mind like a chalice.
I have not disappeared. I swish the amber
hue of lager on my tongue and ponder the drilling
rigs in the Gulf of Alaska and all the oil-painted plovers.

When we talk about limits, we disappear.
In Jasper, Texas you can disappear on a strip of gravel.

I am a life in sacred language.
Termites toil over a grave,
and my mind is a ravine of yesterdays.
At a glance from across the room, I wear
September on my face,
which is eternal, and does not disappear
even if you close your eyes once and for all
simultaneously like two coffins.

Mighty Pawns

If I told you Earl, the toughest kid
on my block in North Philadelphia,
bowlegged and ominous, could beat
any man or woman in ten moves playing white,
or that he traveled to Yugoslavia to frustrate the bearded
masters at the Belgrade Chess Association,
you'd think I was given to hyperbole,
and if, at dinnertime, I took you
into the faint light of his Section 8 home
reeking of onions, liver, and gravy,
his six little brothers fighting on a broken love seat
for room in front of a cracked flat-screen,
one whose diaper sags it's a wonder
it hasn't fallen to his ankles,
the walls behind doors exposing sheetrock,
the perfect O of a handle, and the slats
of stairs missing where Baby-boy gets stuck
trying to ascend to a dominion foreign to you and me
with its loud timbales and drums blasting down
from the closed room of his cousin whose mother
stands on a corner on the other side of town
all times of day and night, except when her relief
check arrives at the beginning of the month,
you'd get a better picture of Earl's ferocity
after-school on the board in Mr. Sherman's class,
but not necessarily when he stands near you
at a downtown bus stop in a jacket a size too
small, hunching his shoulders around his ears,
as you imagine the checkered squares of his poverty
and anger, and pray he does not turn his precise gaze
too long in your direction for fear he blames
you and proceeds to take your Queen.

Stand Your Ground: A Double Golden Shovel

America, how often I have applauded your flagpoles. We,
as citizens, struggle to find common ground, yet do
much to damage the planks of your Ark. Not
a soft tune we make, glissando of the harmonized. We have a want
problem: more of ourselves problem, *Us* versus *Them*
in the great race to prosperity. In his *Introduction to
Metaphysics*, Heidegger asks "Why are there beings at all?" We have
as guides: Klansmen and eugenicists, who proclaim all others are less.
It is, I admit, the slapping of your ropes tolling a perfect union. But,
is the measure of your worth a silent clang elsewhere? How is it
a ripple also runs through *me* when your wind rises? Your cloth is
nation, hauled down or half-mast, like a deferred dream only
earthly because we strive on a path hidden by dead leaves, a natural
entity whose death makes valid its rebirth,—that
an angry man can shoot a teenager is par, as we say. We,
Iota, Deltas, Crips, Knights, new tribesmen in new codes, should
in earnest put away our swords and talk shows. Think:
our watermelons have so many seeds, and we,
galaxy in us, dissolve our supernovas. The mysteries we have,
an unmitigated burning of sound and fury, not
organism of one, but organs. America, I've had enough.

Thinking of Our Shame at the Gas Pump

After nights of strobe lights spinning
hollow festive moods, after listening
to the vast embroidery of our loneliness
at Vagabond or The G Lounge,
after pursuing a private pain mornings
on subways heading home as I read Russian
history and pretended to walk among
a grove of winter trees, hoping to elude
the snarling, mangy dogs roaming
the streets between Girard and Fairmont,
I let two kinds of time pass through me
and shunned the dying madness of corners,
idling cars exchanging Franklins
and Jacksons for delicious bags of cocaine
as if all noses were peasants turned Bolsheviks.
If a correct revolution of minds had come,
I was ready to banish all evidence of myself,
to escape the bright spoors of shell-top
Adidas hanging like testes over power lines.

I now find myself unable to stare across
two islands of gas pumps and advertisements
for *Big Gulps* at my neighbors' shame,
the big whooshing wind of petrol cleansing us
like a complex pattern of synthesizers
and drum machines, a composed miracle
from the saints of progress and commerce.
When we pray, our hands carry the scent
of gasoline, which confuse our brains' God spot
like the brutally noble monks who publicly
claimed their end and set themselves aflame
in protest, an act replicated in Richard

Linklater's film *Waking Life*. Yet now,
also my dream: that irascible man
sanctimoniously reasoning society's
craving for chaos and destruction
before dousing himself with a devil-red
gas can, then cross-legged on a street corner,
lighting a match as though he were
taking a bath of fire, his charred limbs
collapsing into a heap of embers.
To the question "Do you have any last words?"
before being euthanized by injection,
the *New York Times* reported Thomas Youk
as saying, "I never understood a thing,"
and then slumped, his head lolling
to one side like a baby's except forever.

I have friends each year who attend *Burning Man*
in Black Rock Desert. They like having sex
in the semi-arid, alkali flats of northern Nevada,
their bodies blurring to ashes like forty-foot
wooden effigies in a swirling dust, eddying up
and marrying to the vast ritual of ruin
and devastation we seem to have made.
Such public performances, such dissent,
our flailing in discotheques, the bonfire
we make of our bodies is, sure, the irrepressible
blaze of the human, but I read, too, all desire
for meaning abandoned as the flames flare
around us, the startling conclusion
of our perpetual obliviousness.
The islands where we refuel offer temporary
clarity: hose, hole, cap, and go. The shame
we all know is we all leave empty.

Aubade

You could be home, boiling a pot
of tea as you sit on your terrace,
reading up on last night's soccer shot
beneath a scarf of cirrus.

You could be diving headlong
into the waves of Cocoa Beach
or teaching Mao Tse-tung
whose theories are easy to reach.

Or dropping off your dry cleaning,
making the New Americans wealthier,
or mowing your lawn, greening
up, but isn't this healthier?

Just imagine the hours you're
not squandering away,
nor the ant-like minutes frittered
with a tentative fiancé.

Your whole body agrees you'd
rather lie here like a snail
in my arm's crook, nude
and oblivious to all emails.

Yes, it's nearly one o'clock.
But we have more reasons
to kiss, to engage in small talk.
For one, these blissful seasons

are short, & tomorrow is never
insured, so bounce downstairs:
pour us glasses of whatever,
a tray of crackers, Bosc pears,

then let drop your sarong,
the wind high on your skin,
so we can test all day long
the notion of original sin.

Special Needs

Only the skin runs ahead like a spruced-up
dream from which I never awake.
What really exists, no one knows.
In exchange for shook foil,
Hopkins killed the agnostic in him.
I want to kill the polygamist in me.
A sound, a whole sound is never a separation.
A whole sound is an angelic order.
I am most whole in an alley off Market Street
where I pretend to be a sentence
and not a sentiment, a friend to stray
cats and beautiful women. My young cousins only want
hard words and money. If the economy sinks, they will
kill you quicker than a brainwave.
I give my sympathy to the last evangelical.
As long as the body is blaring,
we avoid the straitjackets of conformity.
I am zealous for the taste of my life.
Sometimes, I do not sleep for days.
In the mornings, I rub my hands together
back and forth summoning the angels
away from the orthodoxy of façades.
I reach for the peppershaker
on my spice rack and recall all the pimps
of Chelsea and all the johns on Wall Street.
I see joggers in the street and they remind me
of my most treasured liaisons.
Some men are simply malefic and fall
through your window, wanting to be a part
of something good.

Night Steps

I'll never forget the wind the corner whispered,
nor the windowed darkness that was more
a frame for the world's high-rise loneliness.
I'll never forget the days we lingered
beneath our fingerprints and how we were
each other's private sacrament.
Brooms and mops hung behind doors
like secret agents. The crooks of our knees
ached from all the praying; our astonished hands
could not keep up, being daydreamers
of water towers and such. What monastery would
welcome such afterimages like those we spoke?
Electric wires over a bus stop, a fly mumbling
and dodging a swatter, a light brown maid smiling
on a bottle of corn syrup. I'll never forget
such sprigs of trembling and honeysuckle
nor other forms of desire: the night steps
of an upright bass or blue eyeshadow
like slashes beneath my mother's brow.

On Cocoa Beach

I am revisiting the idea of Florida, giving my vertebrae
a vacation from all the faded bouquets of urine in New York
and the darkened policies of snow in Vermont.
I am revisiting the idea of my wife's imperial gaze;
her three-cheese quiche and fluted mimosas
are the masters of my mornings.
I am revisiting the idea of lawn furniture.
By late afternoon on Sunday my face blossoms
like a passion of lilies as I admire the spectral grace
of the sandhill crane or am caught lost thinking of Castillo
de San Marcos and the first people Timucua.
I am revisiting the idea of light and laughter and skin,
half-transported by wind. I like to think of myself
beside the crepe myrtle pondering the logos
of palm leaves and the kindnesses of beaches.
You can have your sororities of pain and darkened subways.
I will give myself to the great battles of clouds and surfs.

Enchanters of Addison County

We were more than gestural, close-listening,
the scent of manure writing its waft on the leaves
off Route 22A. By nightfall, our gaze flecked
like loon cries, but no one was up for turnips
nor other roots, not least of which the clergy.
Romanticism has its detractors, which is why
we lined the road with tea-lit luminaries
and fresh-cut lemons. We called it making magic,
then stormed the corners and porches
of general stores, kissing whenever cars idled
at four-way stop signs or sought Grade A maple syrup
in tin containers with painted scenes of horse-drawn
farmers plowing through snow. The silhouetted, rusted
farm equipment gave us the laid-back heaven
we so often wished, and fireflies bequeathed earth stars,
such blink and blank and bunk-a-bunk-bunk.
And of course we wondered if we existed,
and also too, the cows of the ancient pastures,
and the white milk inside our heads
like church spires and ice cream cones.
Even after all of that cha-cha-cha, we still came
out of swimming holes shivering our hearts out.

Energy Loves Here

Sun Ra and His Black Magic Soul Power Arkestra, 2014

Clumsily, so In,
those squares—
such states
of Normalcy,

never to feel
the infinite number
of vibratory ratios.
What I play:

Moonwords for
posterity, north
by Northwest
of the Sea of

Fecundity.
Let me find
Beings like myself
lurking in the

Between-ness
of the Kingdom
of Not. All
creations

are music, the
hopeless retelling:
freedom's birth.
Far clouds

like a face,
and each face
an expedition
in sonic justice.

Go on: play your
mug. Make the boom
boom of the New Thing
where a clock is a crime.

Space is not
your death's cave,
but the lights
turned out in

your mind.
If you stand in
the light of an
interplanetary

church, tenderest
effigy of yourself,
then you, too, can
spar with meteors

or memory. Blow
back the ordinary
jive of planet
Earth: my being

is Beingness,
myth business
like man; every
beginning is

a trauma.
Other Planes
of There we seek:
loss as a kind
of predestination.
In the blades of grass,
mourning. I lie
on midnight's

back, conjuring
equations, hoping
some ear decodes
the rhythmic

figures, futuristic
sounds, outer
darkness music,
black music

orbiting your
neoclassical beam
waves. How is
your life art if

you keep playing easy listening
inside your
tomb? Asymmetrical
deviations?

When Angels
Speak of Love,
primitive What's
and How's,

the research
and treatment
of cosmic voids.
We aliens have

little memory
which isn't
reality but the
spacecraft

you know as Life.
What it is? Ultra
Beings in the Space
Gallery, I reach

for your feelings
not your brains.
I don't care who
you are, but what

you can be. Man
is limited. This
is celestial
communication

success. Go on.
Walk Across
the Void. Spaceport
Spirit Sound.

Why I Write Poetry

Because my son is as old as the stars
Because I have no blessings
Because I hold tangerines like orange tennis balls
Because I sit alone and welcome morning across
    the unshaved jaws of my lawn
Because the houses on my street sleep like turtles
Because the proper weight of beauty was her eyes
    last night beneath my eyes
Because the red goblet from which I drank
    made even water a Faustian toast
Because radishes should be banned, little pellets that they are
Because someone says it's late and begins to rise from a chair
Because a single drop of rain is hope for the thirsty
Because life is ordinary unless you plan
    and set in motion a war
Because I have not thanked enough
Because my lips moisten whenever I hear Mingus's
    "Goodbye Pork Pie Hat"
Because I've said the word dumbfuck too many times in my life
Because I plant winter vegetables in July
Because I could say the morning died like candle wax
    and no one would question its truth
Because I relished being sent into the coatroom
    in third grade where alone, I would turn off the light
    and run my hands over my classmates' coats
    as if playing tag with their bodies
Because once I shoplifted a pair of Hawaiian shorts
    and was caught at the Gallery Mall.
Because soup reminds me of the warmth
    of my grandmother and old aunts
Because the long coast of my dreams is filled
    with saxophones and poems

Because somewhere someone is buying a Rolex or a Piaget
Because I wish I could speak three different languages
    but have to settle for the language of business and commerce
Because I used to wear paisley shirts and herringbone sports jackets
Because I better git it in my soul
Because my grandfather loved clean syntax,
    cologne, Stacy Adams shoes, Irish tweed caps,
    and women, but not necessarily in that order
Because I think the elderly are sexy
    and the young are naïve and brutish
Because a vision of trees only comes to
    wise women and men who can fix old watches
Because I write with a pen whose supply of ink comes from the sea
Because gardens are fun to visit in the evenings
    when everyone has put away their coats and swords
Because I still do not eat corporate French fries or rhubarb jam
Because punctuation is my jury and the moon is my judge
Because my best friend in fourth grade chased
    city buses from corner to corner
Because his cousin's father could not stop looking
    up at the sky after his return from the war
Because parataxis is just another way of making ends meet
Because I have been on a steady diet of words
    since the age of three.

FROM
The Absurd Man
(2020)

Major and I

      hand in hand remove our dark suits, but
the other Major prefers to undress in glass
revolving doors; he is a fan of prohibition
cocktails whose potions afford him time-travels
of the landed gentry. I let Major sport
his dangers, which magnify his ambitions
so he can write his grandiloquent poems,
and thus, ours is a compromised relationship:
I, more cautious than a slug, and he,
the sampler of pythons.
      Major is a fan of Peruvian folk songs,
wood-paneled libraries, rare colognes, and old
issues of *Esquire*. I, on the other hand, prefer
American football, treasury bills, and vintage
sports cars. Only once did I try to escape
his clutches, this other Major.
      For years I survived his rank
songs which make the Spanish cantors weep.
His fingers carry the bitter taste of coffee,
which, occasionally, I sniff for they are
the color of ancient bark. Forgive his pretenses, he
who wrote that last sentence. It is probably
true he wrote most of this, but I am unsure
for I live just behind him, a single keystroke
shy of his many thoughts. Beware
his black rituals.
      The other Major flies in his daydreams
which means he's collecting a paradise
of mirrors where I sit studying the prose
of Toomer, Morrison, and Faulkner. Latinate
though he is, master of the outside, he digs
the gangster lean and is more thankful

than a sunroof top. His broken strings, like
his stubble, issue forth a wintry path
at night for white walls. See what I mean?
    Major never won attendance awards,
and for sure long ago he left behind
cigarettes and the guarded strips of lotto
tickets but cherishes still the big hit. Admit
his charms and you've a friend for life.
He will send you sunflowers (true),
even from his coffin (not true), and although
he never learned to play the violin or the mouth
harp, a radio plays like an all-night laundromat
behind his eyes, and thus, he lives year-round
in the boot camp of self-redemption;
for this the other Major needs lots
of sky. You are that sky.

You, Reader

So often I dream of the secrets of satellites
and so often I want the moose to step
from the shadows and reveal his transgressions,
and so often I come to her body
as though she were Lookout Mountain,
but give me a farmers' market to park my martyred masks
and I will name all the dirt roads that dead-end
at the cubist sculpture called *My Infinity*,
for I no longer light bonfires in the city of adulterers
and no longer smudge the cheeks of debutantes
hurriedly floating across the high fruit of night,
and yes, I know there is only one notable death in any small town
and that is the pig farmer, but listen, at all times
the proud rivers mourn my absence, especially
when, like a full moon, you, reader, hidden behind a spray
of night-blooming, drift in and out of scattered clouds
above lighthouses producing their artificial calm,
just to sweep a chalk of light over distant waters.

The Flâneur Tends a Well-Liked Summer Cocktail

curbside on an Arp-like table. He's alone
of course, in the arts district as it were, legs folded,
swaying a foot so that his body seems to summon
some deep immensity from all that surrounds:
dusk shadows inching near a late-thirtyish couple debating
the post-galactic abyss of sex with strangers,
tourists ambling by only to disappear into the street's gloomy mouth,
a young Italian woman bending to retrieve
a dropped MetroCard, its black magnetic strip facing up,
a lone speckled brown pigeon breaking from a flock of rock
doves, then landing near a crushed fast-food wrapper
newly tossed by a bike messenger, the man chortling
after a sip of flaxen-colored beer, remembering
that in the Gospel of John the body and glory converge
linked to incarnation and so, perhaps, we manifest each other,
a tiny shower of sparks erupting from the knife sharpener's
truck who daily leans a blade into stone, a cloudscape reflected
in the rear windshield of a halted taxi where inside
a trans woman applies auburn lipstick, the warlike
insignia on the lapel jacket of a white-gloved
doorman who opening a glass door gets a whiff
of a dowager's thick perfume and recalls baling timothy
hay as a boy in Albania, the woman distractedly watching
a mother discuss Robert Colescott's lurid appropriations
of modernist art over niçoise salad, suddenly frees her left breast
from its cup where awaits the blossoming mouth of an infant
wildly reaching for a galaxy of milk, the sharp coughs
of a student carrying a yoga mat, the day's last light edging
high-rises on the West Side so that they seem rimmed
by fire just when the man says, And yet, immense the wages
we pay boarding the great carousel of flesh.

Going into Battle

The birthmark on the lower right
of my wife's back is a letter of resurrection.
Each night I kiss it before I turn out the lights
so that it blesses my sleep.

A stamp of all her sorrows,
I regard it with the utmost importance,
for it sets her apart from all other creatures.
Sometimes I put my face to its amoeba-like shape
to see if I can hear the long wail of her creation.

Periodically it guides me across the waters
of my absent desire like a beacon,
only brown and lightly spotted.

One before saw it as a sign of war and created a sentinel
around his body, and he who beheld it next heard
the rattling of dice in a gambler's hand.

I am the only one who makes peace before facing
the large screen of dreams, knowing a wind-cursed
city lies behind my eyelids.

The Flag of Imagination Furled

In the middle of March, the sky over Siena
faded like a roar but not the tenants
of cemeteries, for I had not learned to wrestle
the hours nor solved the great riddles
in the narrow districts of my glass-encased cities.
What overcame me, all that running my forefinger
down the wintry pages of my masters
and my adversaries, touching
their sentences like sculptured palaces,
touring their villages of ink? I'm sure
Nina Simone was there and helped to deepen
the pouches beneath my eyes even in gleeful Madrid,
even as I preached to a cloistered community, close-knit
as a garlic clove, or spray-painted morning fog, avoiding
the lash of geraniums lest it launch me into a spell
of lyric wonder. Severe sadness? A cocoon of oppression?
Nothing accounted for my frozen laughter in the proud
cantinas, my meticulous lack of holy clamor as I scribbled
towards some infinitude. How often I've wanted to
cruise my mirrors or pose questions to my footsteps,
of course without the crisis of caves or politicians
eating hungrily from their dark bowls of pocket watches.
There is, within me, an invincible summer,
a seasonal wind, and my name is on it.

.

November in Xichang

> There are cities one won't see again.
>
> *Joseph Brodsky*

1.

Only a bearded smile shows below a conical hat
turning men to rice farmers or Wang Lung pulling
a rickshaw except I'm on a bamboo raft
guided by a soundless Charon whose wooden pole
dips into the Qionghai, spiking dead lotus
flowers. Were this pottery from one of those dynasties,
Ming or Han, there'd be a pagoda, an arching bridge, and us
on a blue and white plate in silk robes, practicing pieties,
forever gazing, as on Keats's urn, though ravished in dry reeds.

2.

The mountains shy at my early arrival, clouds like tangled
lingerie still skirting their range. Up to ankles
in sedge grass, a discouraged heron gawkily aims
for a higher floor then gives a raspy cluck, declaiming
in birdspeak, "There goes the neighborhood."
I want to embrace this scene for all its good,
yet how, with you hotel-bound, coughing, bedridden?
The lake's quiet surface enters my spine, the hidden
marvels suddenly made visible like a torch from a flame.

3.

That stilled fisherman inked to a shadow inhabits
a hanging scroll I've made in my mind,
his back to net and rods, a panel perhaps in classic
script, ideograms spelling out the swiftness of time,
vertically, of course, as he tries to stare
pass weed muck into a future obscured,
as we are, by an understory of shriveled lily pads,
by reflection of an osier's spilling hair. You've had
it with crumpled tissues piling up like drafts.

4.

You've had it with traditional healing teas,
cigarette smoke dragoning through walls.
You've had it with squatting stalls
but not the hospitality of the Yi,
their rotating trays, lamb's tongue, hot pots,
beef and bladder, old-style songs, folk
dances, the falsetto notes of the men, the pitch
of cool in poncho-frayed white cloaks,
the ways to say "beautiful" in everyone's thoughts.

5.

Last night I proclaimed art as a container
for the self on a panel echoing Whitman
then worried I too loudly banged the drum.
Our Chinese friends, tolerant of my campaign
for a spirit radiant as the gold on their flag, clapped
like flickering stars at the end of my speech.

Today, I calm my fears: spy movies, wiretaps,
casual surveillance, the feeling of being watched,
the terrors that enter the room while we sleep.

6.

We steel ourselves despite the filigreed
air, sunlight rendering more real the horror,
our cameras pointing to blood gushing like water
in a rural courtyard. Circled around a table,
our senses empty as fast as lacquer goblets fill.
Nearby, behind a cage, preparing himself for the playbill
featuring himself, a pig practices his squealing
last act. New Year's Day, "Ku Shi" in Yi,
six invisible days but first a slaughter.

7.

In theater seats, in the outdoor air of night,
our eyes focus on a water curtain, a projected eagle
flapping slow-motion: choreographed flames ignite
Heaven's Fire: The Totem of Life but I find its sequel
later in our room without the flashing lights or fountains
shooting their aquatic cannons. What synchronizes
beneath sheets like a lunar eclipse, a *Fragrance
of Years*, a wish, when one partner dies
and the other no longer hears a peacock's screeching cry.

8.

Our wish for faith leads us to Quan Yin visible
on the horizon above village houses. Off tour

we pass through narrow streets seeking her temple,
then plant sticks of incense like flags, give our
three prostrations and pray for compassion.
An old woman whose creases long ago marbled
her face speaks gentle as coiled smoke. I imagine
her blessing us, strangers in her land who marvel
at the slightest kindness, evidence of a human circle.

9.

Though air around us feels like a shrine,
we become creatures of the treaties
of gestures, seeking nonverbal speech to rhyme
with our curiosities, faces that unlock cities
so the massive doors of indifference swing open
and what's revealed, a bright garden that leads toward
some miracle of air. In the Yi Slavery Museum, a Bimo's
screeching dispossession of cries and words
reminds me: we have only each other in the end.

My Children's Inheritance

A fancy for high green hills by a sea, baggy spaces
    in the day, a knack for gunpowder thinking,
a library humming like a swarm of gnats;

the intrigue of a woman with a pitch-perfect mind,
    blinking eyes whose silence is ancient and naked,
a grave, which is not a grave, but a ruin to visit in middle age;

a chifforobe of half-empty cologne bottles in various colors
    and dried flowers more dignified in death, both
evidence that I once cherished bouquets and timelessness;

bullet casings, a bowl of seashells, fine pens, one
    the *Aurora Diamante* with its two-toned rhodium plating
that glitters when my right hand rages toward heaven;

a love of big plates of pasta, Argentinian folk music,
    African rainforests and the speeches of Lincoln that
mist the pages of my books more than my doorways;

a habit of dancing when the needle drops its existential beats,
    a disregard for the enemies of linnets and macaws,
fears that match the hawk-haunted buttes out west;

a hard desire for justice, the habit of lip-biting when trouble
    nears, the way my mouth opens like a flower, my quiver
of arrows that outweighs the world, leaving the animals

to bear witness; memories of laughter that was bread and water,
    stylish hats, ways to time-travel, the consequences
of mistakes and second thoughts gummed to the future;

a collection of radios, stacks of vinyl, the limitations
    of secrets, long nights that cascade like waterfalls,
my madness, granular and complex, sealed like a footfall.

A Brief Reflection on Torture near the Library of Congress

Shouldering a bag of great literature, you glimpse spider silk
extruding from spinnerets, spiraling into
an orb above a restaurant's *Exit* sign. Revenue questions
aside, a diplomat's diamond shirt-studs
sparkle beside Ritzenhoff Cristal just when you recall
bike-riding as a child behind a laundry truck,
its bouquets of lavender spraying the road.

Innocuous the lightness of transactions,
exchanging hands, cash touching in meetings.
Some memories are made for the hatchet's blade.
But the dissidents are rioting today, and a cable station away
above the bar in slow motion a player tosses chalk
into the air like a spell and suddenly you smell
newly opened wads of fresh paper bills.

Yours is the study of steam or how the mind
sprinklers, presently irrigating. Somewhere,
someone is screaming for holy intervention
in a military prison. Once, below a cathedral
of trees with signs along the road that read
Chutes de branches, you pictured a torture table.
The bag now feels like a century of offenses.

The Cloistered Life of Nuns

In Reading Market, you recall a fisherman in Sifnos
fetch a snapper sloshing in a tub, the quick motions
of snipping needlepoint fins, and, tail to head,
rake with the back side of a fillet knife
so that little translucent scales seem to burst
like a frenzy of designs from the Age of Enlightenment.

The mind sweeps empty opening into night.

A poacher hacks the face of an elephant and
tugs at ivory tusk as the driver listens
to Ragamuffin while reading Job 40:15.

Suppose there is an Architect or a Gnostic,
what consciousness could we ever possess?
What then of the discontents rioting today?
On a spatial scale, Plato held the ideal
Republic should glimmer into sight.

A German shepherd barks at a rabbit secreted in a hedgerow
over genial chatter at a Hamptons summer party
as water striders dogpaddle on a man-made pond in sync.
The carnage as a way of life like a plain gold
ring inscribed with a single word: Darwin.

You touched a peach and saw in your mind
the cloistered life of nuns descending
stairwells like moths. So much crushed ice
spilling out of crates on the floor,
stilled fish eyes marbling.

Behold now behemoth, which I made with thee; he eateth grass as an ox.

My Son and Me

At the bar in Otto's near Fifth,
both off from work, the heavy
foot traffic of silhouetted commuters
hastening home outside, and us, here
two drinks in. The conversation
has just ramped up and he wants
to know why I did it, how I could have betrayed
our family. The bartender is in night school,

we learn, for law, but, meanwhile, he can name
all the great vineyards in Sonoma,
and how many laborers worked the field
and how many the crush pad
last planting season which incidentally he says
gave us some of the best varietals,
he's told, in years: "But it's all really
just a racket though like anything else in life."

I want to tell my son about the great poems
I've taught today yet careful to avoid
the sad lives of the poets, but he has long been
exhausted of lines I recited to him since a child,
my eyes carrying the exuberance of art, and so
would only agitate and call up his condemnation
of my friends as shams parading their
pain as pomp. Instead, I reach for

his hand across the varnished oak top:
"I was disappearing" to which he shakes
his head. I swirl my glass, looking down avidly,
churning the air so as to deliver oxygen
and open up the wine, wishing to
release its veiled bouquet.

I've Said Too Much

I've said too much. The soil overruns with honey.
Porch lights blaze into the afternoons.
I find it difficult to control my idioms; only ask
which direction the wind blows,
and I will give you a history of my elms and
cottonwoods or my theft of fire. My brain plunders
its orchard of speech. Watch the expressionist stains
at the corners of my mouth, dark as blueberries,
blossom into a symphony. I am too far from the land
of hush to be useful. What is said must be said
so I say it. Inheritor of hieroglyphs and cave drawings,
I keep the engines of hearsay fueled,
an echo of the ancients, especially the Sophists.
Leave me with your griefs and barefoot secrets,
and rest assured, I will secure your memory,
and your name, the tremble of a wave heading
to shore will ricochet back into the deep sea
of my sayings and bewilderments. Provide a backdrop
of cheese and tapenades with a little sauvignon
from the Cederberg Mountains and you can have
a lifetime of constellations as you take in the great stone
korai at the Acropolis of Major, unyielding in slanting light.

The Body's Uncontested Need to Devour: An Explanation

I am bathing again, burying my face
into the great nations of moss.
I am leaning in, smelling the emerald mountains
and the little inhabitants crossing
over rock-like boulders and tree trunks empired
bit by bit. My nose must come to them
like a probing spaceship causing a mighty eclipse.
They speak in whispers but do not shriek
when gazing into the dim landing bays
of my cavernous thoughts. I am grazing
like a Dionysian. I come not with religion.
I come yearning for first spring and a thirst for spores
pooling like mercenaries in the dark, even as we speak.
The little gods of the forest live here.
I want to ingest their verdant settlements
until they carpet my cavities and convert my raptorial
self into its own ecosystem, off into the green.

Vermont Eclogue

Damp patches of mountain fog. Late afternoon
country roads clamoring for sleep.
Light snow, patient as an assassin, through
leafless branches mists your car.
African masks with half-closed eyes
on a living room wall seem disoriented.
House lights flash on like strong-scented
signals. Below, two moles cross a paddock in
opposite directions. A transient sculpture
of blue jays vaults toward a cluster
of white pines. Behind the thickening sky,
the peaks are shy as migrants.
Earbuds fastened in, you sing, *don't disturb
this groove*, your voice its own woodland
where a man stands at the edge
of a pond watching crystals dissolve in midair.

Winter

The boughs have been naked for weeks.
Snowplows scrape the highway clean of its sugar.
People withdraw into their nests and study
the language of fire. A group of high school girls
on their way home in the afternoon dark
fall into an embankment and flap their arms
and legs as though cloud-swimming towards the coming world.
The blank silence of dead earth forces us
to gaze up, harvest the black music that belongs
to all the eyes in the future who will also turn to the spheres
and study too whatever light to fill their emptiness.

Dear Zaki

like a stream of wet gold floats by my face his words are
like that
for Ntozake Shange (1948–2018)

Thoughts today
of you emerged as I walked
the streets, somewhat frayed
& distraught by more hearsay
of another poet's passing—

this time Gregg
with whom I once shared a beer
after a gig in the Village.
Shamelessly I pelted her
I recall about Gilbert, Grecian

islands, landscapes
that crack both pen & heart.
Despite my bantering & poor taste,
Linda indulged the young upstart
hungry for gossip, our parade

of mistakes. Yet,
what she gave were lessons
on being true to the calling, none
of the angers some
shape into being undone,

but a gratitude
for mornings of coffee
brewed in a briki pot, views
of the Aegean, waves of blue.
his shrill eyes. Glued

to her voice,
I ran a finger along the scarred,
oak table, carvings of a couple rejoic
-ing in the fresh chords
of a new love wishing to foist

their joys on
(the lonely? the fallen?)
unsuspecting tenants
in that dark bar: *Dylan
+ Diane Forever* within

cupid's arrow.
Her mascara was thick
as a Kollwitz, a heavy sorrow
rivering beneath drift
-ing memories of her Romeo.

The world's full
of absurd men, free
of guilt, whose kisses are lures
that hook a would-be bride then flee
leaving musky trails, vapor

-ous hopes, ruined
bodies, the marked scents of beasts,
closed eyes singing bloodlines,
their love of mirrors & creaky
beds. *Her* news reminded

I'd yet named
my debt to you. Once,
David Murray, in concert, claimed
the Painted Bride stage, his famed
Afro-horn found the pulse

223

of the crowd
&, like *Probe*, blew extensions,
to which, behind shades, in loud
leopard print, ignoring the too-proud,
you swayed like a palm tree. When

*The Love Space
Demands* staged the next weeks
I sought local places
you ate, restaurants & boutiques.
I sought your plays, your books,

your nappy
edges, hipster spirit, boho
freedom, you who spoke the holy
order of black poems, so
in the vernacular of us, the tempo

of good-foot
rhythms & wadings in secret
creeks. I felt baptized when you put
in my hands Blakey's Quartet
A Jazz Message at the record

store on 3rd
out of the blue. Of course
you lived in *The Chocolate Works*,
you who would talk Karl Marx,
mamboed from Flatbush to the Bronx.

And all we,
bippies, divas, & black bohos
discussed was you: Zaki
at gallery openings; Zaki
in clubs striking poses.

When you died,
dusk inside eyes everywhere
like Bastille lost Baudelaire,
& the women who feared
rainbows fading from skies,

rubbed out by
the erasers of gray clouds,
lost their dance. Yet, my profound
paradox: I, too, caused enough cry
-ing women to fill a sky.

A young man,
my ambivalence was wide.
I claimed as many as my hands
could hold. Teary-eyed,
their love slammed

into my need
to be loved endlessly
like Christmas all the time. A greed
born of the ego? or a reckless
allegiance to the now? I received

all manner
of guidance from brilliant
women like you, but my pattern
of love-them-then-leave-them
ignored hearts. What use then

this thunder
in the mountains? I've learned
to translate silence, to live under
my own body, the unending alarm
of so much suffering.

You knew far
more about the wounds
of men no north star
could heal. We're bound to earth
and wear each other's scars.

In Memory of Derek Alton Walcott

I.

Island traffic slows to a halt
as screeching gulls reluctant
to lift heavenward
congregate like mourners in salt-
crusted kelp as the repellent
news spreads to colder shores:

Sir Derek is no more.
Bandwidths, clogged by streaming
tributes, carry the pitch
of his voice, less so his lines, moored
as they are to a fisherman's who strains
in the Atlantic

then hearing too drops his rod, the reel
unspooling like memory till
his gaped mouth matches
the same look in his wicker creel,
that frozen shock, eyes marble
a different catch.

Pomme-arac trees, sea grapes,
and laurels sway, wrecked having lost
one who heard their leaves'
rustic dialect as law, grasped
their bows as edicts from the first
garden that sowed faith,—

and believe he did, astonished
at the bounty of light, like Adam,
over Castries, Cas-
en-Bas, Port of Spain, the solace
of sonorous rains, clouds like hymns
then edens of grass,

ornate winds on high verandahs
carrying spirits who survived
that vile sea-crossing,
who floated up in his stanzas,
the same souls Achille saw alive,
the ocean their coffin,—

faith, too, in sunsets, horizons
whose backlit job is to divide
and spawn reflection
which was his pen's work, reason
twinned with delight, divining
like a church sexton.

Poetry is empty without
discipline, without piety,
he cautions somewhere,
even his lesser rhymes amount
to more than wrought praise but amplify
his poems as high prayer.

So as to earn their wings above,
pelicans move into tactical
formation, then fly
low like jet fighters in honor of
him, nature's mouth, their aerial
salute and goodbye.

II.

Derek, each journey we make
whether Homeric or not
follows the literal wake
of some other craft's launch,

meaning to sense the slightest
motions in unmoving waters
is half the apprentice's
training before he oars

out, careful to coast, break
-ing English's calm surface.
What you admired in Eakins
in conversation at some café

(New Orleans? Philly?) was
how his rower seemed to listen
to ripples on the Schuylkill as
much as to his breath, both silent

on his speaking canvas.
Gratitude made you intolerant
of the rudeness of the avant-
garde or any pronouncements

of the "new," for breathing is
legacy and one's rhythm,
though the blood's authentic
transcription, hems us

to ancestors like a pulse. This,
I fathom, is what you meant
when exalting the merits
of a fellow poet: That man

is at the center of language,
at the center of the song.
Yet a reader belongs to another age
and, likely to list our wrongs

more than the strict triumphs
of our verse, often retreats
like a vanished surf, spume
frothing on a barren beach.

The allure of an artist's works
these days is measured
by his ethics, thus our books,
scrubbed clean, rarely mention

the shadowless dark that settles
over a page like an empire's. Your nib,
like the eye of a moon, flashed into sight
the source of Adam's barbaric cry.

III.

Departed from paradise,
each Nobody a sacrifice,
debating whose lives matter
whereon a golden platter

our eyes roll, dilated by hate
from Ferguson to Kuwait.
You, maître, gave in laughter
but also for the hereafter

an almost unbearable
truth: we are the terrible
history of warring births
destined for darkest earth.

So as fiber optic lights
bounce under oceans our white
pain, codified as they are
and fiber-layered in Kevlar,

we hear ourselves in you,
where time exiles us to
stand lost as a single nation
awaiting your revelations.

A shirtless boy, brown as bark,
gallops along shore, bareback
and free on a horse until he fades,
a shimmering, all that remains.

The Romantics of Franconia Notch

Matthew Dickman and I are fond
of resurrecting the spotted faces
of state troopers and small-town police
we've met over the years.
We love their melodrama, the way they peel
their aviators in the rearview
of my Jetta as they approach
the car like shy teenagers on a first date
then doff their stiff-brim hats with yellow braids.

There was the pastel-loving cop in Eugene
fond of art deco motels in South Beach,
and the comic book fan in Littleton,
New Hampshire who unlatched his gun
holster, and the one tormented by Goethe's
propositions and thus, led us, chorale-like,
through a few hymns before issuing a roadside
warning in Randolph, Vermont.

When they ask us where are we going,
we almost always respond to the town square,
of course, to give the park back to the wretched
men and their brown bags of sorrow and needles
which turn them to black puddles. We want the crime squad
to know we have a purpose, that we sugar our hopes
with the honeyed lines of Brodsky, Pessoa, and Thoreau
whom we were declaiming just that moment,
zipping in the dark, past low-lit Colonials
when a black bear jumped out as though chased
by the ghost of the bear he used to be and Matthew
turned up Jay-Z's *Black Album* so he'd get
a boost and lurch into further darkness.

Urban Renewal

xxvi. Washington Square

When all that cautions the eyes toward the imminent
slide of autumn to arctic winds, the canopy of English elm
and sycamore leaves like colored coins fall and widen
a hole letting more light spill in, heaven's alms
to earth whose ashen gray and white will soon be all the rage,
our guilty secret is the baby grand playing Glass's *Orphée
Suite for Piano*. Nearby Butoh dancers writhe & almost upstage
with white-painted faces of horror (portraits of Nagasaki?),
and past the fountain's water plumes, a drug-riddled couple
shares the smoldering remain of an American Spirit,
their grizzled dog roped to a shopping cart and frayed duffel
bag, this city's updated version of the *American Gothic*.
Our reddish-haired pianist lets the melancholic notes
float to high-rises on Fifth above its triumphal arch,
like a film in reverse where the golden foliage is read by a poet
as autumn's light pours in. "Don't Get Around Much
Anymore," The Ink Spots' Decca cover spins on a phonograph,
an era spiraling soft then held by his gentle pen.

xxvii. Thinking of Frost

I thought by now my reverence would have waned,
matured to the tempered silence of the bookish or revealed
how blasé I've grown with age, but the unrestrained
joy I feel when a black skein of geese voyages like a dropped
string from God slowly shifting, when the decayed
apples of an orchard amass beneath its trees like Eve's
first party, when driving and the road Vanna-Whites its crops
of corn whose stalks will soon give way to a harvester's blade
and turn the land to a man's unruly face, makes me believe
I will never soothe the pagan in me, nor exhibit the propriety
of the polite. After a few moons, I'm loud this time of year,
unseemly as a chevron of honking. I'm fire in the leaves,
obstreperous as a New England farmer. I see fear
in the eyes of his children who walk home from school
as evening falls like an advancing trickle of bats, the sky
pungent as bounty in chimney smoke. I read the scowl
below the smiles of parents at my son's soccer game, their agitation,
the figure of wind yellow leaves make of quaking aspens.

xxviii. Paris

The roaring above rooftops riffed me out
of a sleep so violent I knocked my head,
jolting to snare drums and brass at the outer
reaches of wakefulness. 7:14. I misread
a digital clock, then sprung open our rented
terrace window behind Musée d'Orsay
to see tricolor clouds of France's flag scripted
across the sky over the Champs-Élysées.
Right! Bastille Day. All morning, the marching
of many feet to civic tunes of a country's
pride served as backdrop—some sergeant
in rattling armor and gold epaulettes conducted
when she and I kissed, having survived our clash
of weapons and disloyalties. We had no desire
to gawk with the crowds at passing troops, convoys
of tanks, or watch clumps fall behind cavalries of horse riders.
Instead, I gazed down at her trembling eyelash,
for we had in mind our own drills to stage which garnered
a parade of oohs and aahs, keeping its own cease-fire.

xxix. North Philadelphia

In the solitary, shaded musk of a storefront
church, abandoned save for such secret assembly,
save for slivers of light illuminating drifting motes,
and in the occasional blast across ankles of wintry
air beneath front pews where three women, shawled
and rocking, gathered in a circle late afternoons
as though Sundays were a kind of god crawl,—
there they groaned, repairing from urban fields, tunes
not so much learned yet risen, earth's laments
gardened in throats from black soil, a slow grumbling,
fitful drawn-out grunts grafting onto gospel notes
not recognized but felt, a ring-shout. Poor folk, troubled
by the devil's work through the week: a cheating
husband, a daughter's addiction, one's house
candled from a gambled paycheck, here rich
in spiritual intimacies, the church dark as a hearse.
I'm still in that dimness, several rows behind their wails,
writing their moans coming through like Braille.

xxx. Fish & Wildlife

The lake's cold shacks of ice-fishing anglers
speeds by like homeless shanties. This is North Country,
where a cabin's fireplace wears moose antlers,
where the mesmeric drift of snow snakes Route 30
sending a chalk-white F-150 plummeting into a ditch.
Icicles hover above like liquid spears.
A shawled neighbor in silhouette is a witch
but you believe in the company of man and seek a cold beer
and the crackling fire of a bar up the road whose patrons'
talk of deadly snowmobiles steams its front
window. Gossip turns the evening darker, and the nation
might as well be this small shadowy room half in hunting
gear, eyeing the woman holding a cue at a haloed
pool table. Outside, a grumbling snowplow barrels up
the street like a middle linebacker. A truckload
of modern furniture sits in the parking lot. Yep,
someone says to a Patriots loss: Shoulda won that
one. The almost bare streets seem clutched
in ice, wind dusting up crystals in orange streetlight.
Old men in Franklin County dream of being touched.

xxxi. Double View of the Adirondacks as Reflected over Lake Champlain from Waterfront Park

The mountains are at their theater again,
each ridge practicing an oration of scale and crest,
and the sails, performing glides across the lake, complain
for being outshadowed despite their gracious
bows. Thirteen years in this state, what hasn't occurred?
A cyclone in my spirit led to divorce, four books
gave darkness an echo of control, my slurred
hand finding steadiness by the prop of a page,
and God, my children whom I scarred! Pray they forgive.
My crimes felt mountainous, yet perspective
came with distance, and like those peaks, once keening
beneath biting ice, then felt resurrection in a vestige
of water, unfrozen, cascading and adding to the lake's
depth, such have I come to gauge my own screaming.
The masts tip so far they appear to capsize, keeling
over where every father is a boat on water. The wakes
carry the memory of battles, and the Adirondacks
hold their measure. I am a tributary of something greater.

xxxii. The Valkyrie

The land nearly erased, the mountains flee.
Another arctic blast of snow falls on the peaks
concealing that panorama which first bewitched
my breath where now across the valley wind gusts kick
up land clouds akin to silvery explosions
trip-wired by some aimless deer whose timid motions
break into a sudden sprint across a logging road
then up a gnarled hillside of saplings and dense trees. Slow
wars within begin this way, a vaporous fog
from which I've sought a path out of the monologue
in my head: I've no true friends, my verse's
mediocre at best, a white captivity of rehearsed
caustic thoughts that mist in layers and blind
reason. Then reversing my iceberg mind,
always her with that voice bright as a cardinal
and campfire hands leading me past glacial
snowpiles. Everywhere icicles collect like daggers;
subzero air cuts through harsh as Wagner's
Die Walküre. We've survived blizzard nights,
both of us refunding earth's stolen daylight.

The Absurd Man Suite

> I want to liberate my universe of its phantoms and to people it solely with flesh-and-blood truths whose presence I cannot deny.
>
> *Albert Camus*

The Absurd Man at Fourteen

After church in an empty parking lot one Sunday
facing the Schuylkill, my mother wept
behind a steering wheel. My feet throbbed
in a pair of Buster Browns I'd outgrown
by a season as I looked out the window,
autumn performing its last dying.

He punched her again, a woman called the house,
some yelling then us out the door leaving
the kitchen phone cord swinging.

Morning light burnished the windshield.
Her wet face made her holy. A lone
sculler scissored the river, his silhouette
a shadow in motion. I wanted to say
something but my eyes flamed wild
as the reddish orange leaves firing
up the ground. His stony look as we left
said he was both tormentor and master.

I let her cry, and felt a new world
of women grow around me,
and when she reached for my hand
instinctively I pulled away, her mouth
open to my fading, unbearable heart.

Augustinian

Like a sage walking a dirt road
muddied from an afternoon rain, he feels
less the aristocrat given his threadbare deeds,
his less than noble teeth, the way he squanders
second chances only to excel at a kind of
blind teetering like a mole in a cave.

He accepts rainclouds the way he accepts aspirin.
What is left to be said only that he followed
desire's holy waves Chagall-like across rooftops,
itself a religion, and fastened his embarrassments
to tales of hocus-pocus. Broken whispers
and miles to go. So as not to look pupil-less,

he meditates until peace bubbles
like a bubble on water, glass consciousness.
The laundered napkin, smooth on his lap, turns
His knee to just another white hill.

The Most Beautiful Man Never Performs Hard Labor

I am sure my grandfather would be ashamed
of my hands for they carry nothing and are soft
as downy feathers, and I am sure he'd look
askance at my treasured collection of stemless wine glasses

and fashionable ascots; I am sure he'd smirk at the sight
of fresh cut flowers delivered at my door Tuesday afternoons
when my silken thoughts make like schools of minnows,
and so, too, the cantatas filling my house, and me, paddling

like a dog through the recitatives, so unaccustomed
my hands to the shape and feel of a revolver or the wood
shaving tools he kept in his tool belt like armaments;
I am sure he'd shake his head at my having paused beneath

a fruit tree on a bicycle with a basket, carrying a French baguette
& a collection of Lorca's poetry, angling for a woman's touch.

The Absurd Man on Objet Petit A'

In movies, the bad guy stands-off face
to face with the good guy. They are wanted
in each other's town, but we know
as moviegoers they are the same person
and could win a look-alike contest
if one were more famous than the other.

Our recognition of form and content,
or Lacan's mirror stage, takes us
above the clouds in the late style
of midcentury Dutch chairs
and talk analysis.

The two would do well to lick the other's birthmarks
except for desire is two pistols observed
in an optical field, *mise en abyme*, forming a kind
of blissed-out symmetry,
or so thinks Major.

In a 1970's advertisement, a woman lays
on the glassy hood of a Fiat Spider;
this, too, requires us to stand oblique
to our own image. Ponder, for example,
Holbein's *The Ambassadors*.
Nobody wins.

Oracle & Prophecy

What I learned to endure was not the weight
of an evaporated wallet or squirrelly women improvising
mincing steps across city streets but simply
the mechanical dance of living, and having since learned
the precise count of ballroom steps toward my children, these days,
I stay indoors and watch carpet fibers grow around
my planted feet or dust bunnies gather like a conference
of aspiring clouds outside my bedroom door. This was life
in the vale: amatory flicks conjured in whispered
late-night disclosures scene after inglorious scene.
Picture a spotlight on stage, alone, staring at a low-domed oculus
when sure as stars I was the pedestal and the monument,
the oracle and the prophecy touched by a void.
Yes, one could make a documentary of my running man
or my blues trot, but I'd rather you meet me in the next sentence:
This body is no longer a passing prayer sung by those fearful of time.

How to Avoid a Crash

Some mornings riding to work
on a road bike up a busy thoroughfare,
my hands tight around the handlebars,
I think of my secrets, a slaughterhouse of whispers.

Near the off-ramp, a semitruck's tires squeal
hard up ahead and exhaust fumes nearly blind
as I navigate periodic surges and tons of metal
accelerating by like oversized munitions.

They held tight, like me, full of an emptiness
we so longed to supplant with desire, our muscles
rough pedaling toward an imaginary terminus.

Now I make eye contact, as experts suggest,
with others whose loud music from open windows
or makeup appliqués have no chance
of sending them swerving in my direction,
jarring me off a path I work to keep,
catapulting me, eyes full of terror, over a median
and down the road's unforgiving blacktop.

Our Eyes Are Far Away

Our eyes were far away, as were
the hills writing their own memoirs,
marking our stark absence,
our blue-faced emptiness.

We believed what we felt then
till our doctrines signaled
nothing. Naked, we woke
to our islands and dressed

having canceled the tour.
In the corner, there was a mirror
but the prophets were there
sequestered, withdrawn.

Our sculptures revealed
remote testimonies. Who revolted
as fresh hatreds swept
across our faces while we slept?

We walked past the coffin
of what we once were, the dead
awakened, no longer safe
in our siestas. We thought we said

everything. We hadn't.
Bloodstained, we now raise
a bandaged hand and pen. Where
we want to go has no name.

The Absurd Man in the Mirror

At sunset, winter mountains reach
across a page the color of honey.
Sometimes my hands want
all of her syllables.
I walk in kindness
when she's around
which is to say I feel
Chaplinesque. I mend myself
because she hungers
for golden peaks.
The eastern horizon
offers its diamonds
which we stash
in silent mumblings.
When she speaks, I feel
unburied yet hear still the dead
of my own house. No one cares
that I count her eye blinks.
No one cares about all this hard water.
The hours are tall as polar caps.

Now That You Are Here, I Can Think

What you really are is svelte,
the mainland of your feelings
a young Veronica Webb, and what we share
are solutions, and not so much
the Parisian air you tired of, nor the fat,
sweaty bead coursing a décolletage,
an unlikely consequence of the Kyoto
Protocol, but the pleasures
of lounging below French-style
windows open wide as arms whose blowsy
curtain is a shawl that formally hangs
and informally shifts when you
drift into the room like
a Spike Lee dolly shot.

The kids are dancing to some Ariana,
but I'm watching what you do
with your lips when reading silently
around 4:22 p.m. on a late Sunday afternoon.

I have a weakness for marble winding
stairs and tight two-person elevators.
But the brasseries are waiting
as well as the *fútbol* fans who need help
cheering, for we are Americans after all
and are ready to hype even the locusts on the day
of judgment. I don't care about the midfielder
or the winger. You're smiling, and that's all
the defending I'll ever need.

The Absurd Man Is Subject to Pareidolia

No one believes in angels.
The hills appear lost.
The president waves routinely.
At dusk, the passing towns gather all
their charms and give them to the coming night,
the body's coffin.

The dashboard's panel is a commercial
break from the mind of forest,
music burning in the seeds.

"If not for angels, we'd fall to more wars,"
I say, "and my love weighs
more than the universe.
Don't ask me to explain this."
Car beams fall on the trees.

Something shows between
the branches, taking shape.
I know I'll suffer this plague forever.

Nothing to See Here, Move Along

All through my days, elaborate silken rays
coming through screens carrying
their own occult. I am in the habit of questioning love
which is a storm of rare light
silvering spider webs in a sacred forest,
the silent clock in the town square,
the heavy footprints of the homeless,
the museum we do not enter.

So when I say I've subdued
the stallions raging in my blood,
know that I travel here only to watch
the sparrow hawk flying low over marl prairie,
to take in the sedge wren's flits and jukes
like teenagers learning a new dance.
I'm here guarding my freedom,
rubbing my hands over yesterday fires.

Double Major

I emerge whenever he confuses the lamp for a moon.
It is then he thinks of fine bindings in ordered athenaeums.
I own his face, but he washes and spends too little time behind his ears.
He sees me in the mirror behind thick clouds of shaving
    cream then suddenly believes in ghosts.
His other selves are murals in the cave of his mind. They are speechless
    yet large. They steer his wishes like summer rain and amplify
    his terrors like newscasters.
What he doesn't know: his dreams are his father's dreams, which are his
    grandfather's dreams, and so on. *They* possessed a single wish.
He knocks repeatedly on the bolted door to his imagination.
Tragically, he believes he can mend his wounds with his poetry.
And thus, I am his most loyal critic. He trots me out like a police dog.
He calls our thirst for pads and pencils destiny.
Our voices come together like two wings of a butterfly.
On occasion, he closes his eyes and sees me.
I am negative capability: the test to *all men are created equal*.
We are likely to dance at weddings against my will. He pulled out the same
    moves writing this poem, a smooth shimmy and a hop.
This page is a kind of looking glass making strange whatever stone carvings
    he installed along the narrow road to his interior.
I suffer in silence wedded to his convictions. He would like to tell you
    the truth about love. But we are going to bed, to bed.

Acknowledgments

Thanks to the editors of the following publications where new poems first appeared: Academy of American Poet's *Poem-a-Day*, *The Adroit Journal*, *Ambit Magazine*, *Boston Review*, *Kenyon Review*, *Literary Imagination*, *Orion Magazine*, *Oxford Review*, *Poetry London*, *Prairie Schooner*, *Sewanee Review*, and *World Literature Today*.

"Ode to Everything" appears in the anthology *Best American Poetry 2022*, edited by Matthew Zapruder.

"Double Major" appears in the anthology *Best American Poetry 2021*, edited by Tracy K. Smith.

"Memories of West Fourth Street" appears in the anthology *World Out of Reach: Dispatches from Life under Lockdown*, edited by Meghan O'Rourke.

"Eleutheria" appears in the anthology *Alone Together: Love, Grief, Comfort in a Time of COVID-19*, edited by Jennifer Haupt.

"Invocation" appears in the anthology *Together in a Sudden Strangeness: American Poets Respond to the Pandemic*, edited by Alice Quinn.

"Thinking of Frost" appears in the anthology *Tree Lines: 21st Century American Poems*, edited by Jennifer Barber, Jessica Greenbaum, and Fred Marchant.

"How to Listen" was set to music by composer Gregory W. Brown. The piece was performed by tenor James Reese and pianist Daniel Overly at the Philadelphia Chamber Music Society on April 13, 2022.

"Ferguson," "Euphoria," and "How to Listen" appear in the anthology *African American Poetry: 250 Years of Struggle & Song*, edited by Kevin Young.

Special thanks are owed to my family for their sheer patience and good humor over the years: Didi Jackson, Langston McCullough, Anastasia Nona White, James Welden Romare Jackson (Romie), Dylan Berry, and Lian Jacobs. I should also name our dogs Finn and Buzz (RIP), and our cat Obi.

Poets Aria Aber, Michael Dickman, and L. A. Johnson made crucial contributions to this book. I am grateful for their discerning ears, critical remarks, and conspicuous enthusiasm.

Many of the poems in "Lovesick" first saw light as drafts in my weekly writing group with people who are dear to me: Matthew Dickman, Dorianne Laux, Michael McGriff, Joseph Millar, and Sharon Olds. They return me to the joys of writing poetry when I failingly prioritize all else.

Thanks to my colleagues and friends at Bennington College, New York University, Vanderbilt University, and University of Vermont. Over the years, they, along with my students, have gifted me an astonishing amount of inspiration. They are too numerous to name, but their brilliant literary works and laughter have liberated me from staid orthodoxies.

I am guided by the dazzling displays of erudition and care of my former teachers Sonia Sanchez and Garrett Hongo, *and* by the example and passion of many friends who at some points were more like mentors. As with previous books, this volume of poetry is not possible without them.

Like most artists, I am ever evolving and driven by curiosity and reverence. Recently, my critical outlook on literature has been enriched by conversations with Rabih Alameddine, Victoria Chang, John Freeman, Andrew Greer, Daniel Handler, Robert Hass, Aleksandar Hemon, Brenda Hillman, Ada Limón, and Matthew Zapruder. They are among a group of friends who I owe a special debt of gratitude. Their light and provocations are part of the DNA of this book: Emily Bernard, Reginald Dwayne Betts, Daniel Black, Jay Clayton, Nan Cohen, Rene Colehour, Lydia Conklin, Kate Daniels, Kwame Dawes, Michael Dickman, Camille Dungy, Tony Earley, Jennifer Fay, Tonya Foster, Vievee Francis, John Gennari, Terrance Hayes, Rick Hilles, Randall Horton, Mitchell S. Jackson, Amy and Mark Jarman, Tyehimba Jess, Scott Juengel, A. Van Jordan, Sheba Karim, David Lehman, Emily Lordi, Sebastian Matthews, Gail Mazur, Jill McDonough, Lorrie Moore, John Murillo, Dana Nelson, ZZ Packer, Gregory Pardlo, Ed Pavlić, Willie Perdomo, Sonya Posmentier, Justin Quarry, Anthony Reed, Nancy Reisman, Patrick Rosal, Adam Ross, Jess Row, Allison Schacter, Jason Schneiderman, Salvatore Scibona, Tim Seibles, Prageeta Sharma, Tracy K. Smith, Sandy Solomon, Bianca Stone, Ben Tran, Pádraig Ó Tuama, Afaa Weaver, and Joshua Weiner.

My deepest appreciation extends to my collaborators and friends, artists Jane Kent and Jill Moser, who by sharing their art and passion aided me in finding a pathway into my own.

Eternal gratitude to the members and the vision of The Dark Room Collective and Cave Canem. Love to Chloe Garcia Roberts and Christina Thompson at *Harvard Review*, and Kathy Volk Miller and Marion Wrenn at *Painted Bride Quarterly*. I have been enriched through my work and friendship with Myka Kielbon, Beth Pearlman, and James Napoli at The Slowdown podcast.

I wish to thank all the good folks who build and convene communities of writers. I treasure my affiliation with Cave Canem, Community of Writers, Napa Valley Writers Conference, and Furious Flower Conference. Gratitude to my friends and colleagues at the following organizations who remind me that we must steward the next generation of artists: African Poetry Book Fund, *American Poetry Review*, Cave Canem, Inc, Fine Arts Work Center in Provincetown, *Orion Magazine*, Poetry Society of America, Poets & Writers, Inc., The Porch, and Vermont Studio Center. Please financially support all of the above organizations.

Thank you to the many people, cultural workers, festival organizers, teachers, administrators at high schools, universities and colleges, art centers, and reading groups, who have invited me to talk, lecture, and share my poetry both in the United States, Canada, China, Greece, Hong Kong, Ireland, Jamaica, Mexico, Ireland, Jamaica, and the United Kingdom. Thank you to my booking agency, Blueflower Arts, Inc.

I am grateful, as ever, to my dedicated editor Jill Bialosky and the incomparable team of amazing folks at W. W. Norton, including Drew Elizabeth Weitman, who made possible this book and my four previous books of poetry.

Finally, Didi Jackson's unflagging support and surges of love is its own galaxy. She is my well at the world's end.

Index of Titles & First Lines

Absurd Man at Fourteen, The	240
Absurd Man in the Mirror, The	247
Absurd Man Is Subject to Pareidolia, The	249
Absurd Man on Objet Petit A', The	243
Absurd Man Suite, The	240
A fancy for high green hills by a sea, baggy spaces	211
After church in an empty parking lot one Sunday	240
After nights of strobe lights spinning	184
After Riefenstahl	140
A halyard peals and resounds this clear morning	110
All through my days, elaborate silken rays	250
All we want is to succumb to a single kiss	161
America, how often I have applauded your flagpoles. We,	183
Anacoluthon	27
And though I say here sorrow beguiles me	25
Anthrodrome	151
As a child I wanted as many letters	8
As if every evening your body is a smile	155
As if one day, a grand gesture of the mind, an expired	137
As if the whole inferno. It's a melodrama	159
A soggy brightness at the northernmost ridge	145
At sunset, winter mountains reach	247
At the bar in Otto's near Fifth,	216
Aubade	186
Augustinian	241
Because my son is as old as the stars	196
Beneath canopies of green, unionists marched doggedly	173
Between Two Worlds	78

257

Bless your hallowed hands, Sir, and their paternal blues.	54
Blunts	60
Body's Uncontested Need to Devour: An Explanation, The	219
Brief Reflection on Torture near the Library of Congress, A	213
But the daydream collapses and time returns us	147
By a falling Cyclone chain-	90
By lamplight my steady hand brushes a canvas—	49
Cecil B. Moore	126
Climate	30
Cloistered Life of Nuns, The	214
Clumsily, so In,	192
Cobbled streets have the burnished look of stone skulls	177
Creationism	136
Crossing Over	75
curbside on an Arp-like table. He's alone	204
Damp patches of mountain fog. Late afternoon	220
Dear Gwendolyn—or is it Dear Madam?	102
Dear Zaki	222
Death, but not	75
Designer Kisses	155
Desperate to learn all there was to learn about	17
Door I Open, The	154
Double Major	251
Down here we have inherited an arcade of stars	26
Dynagroove	148
Eleutheria	18
Enchanters of Addison County	191
Energy Loves Here	192
Erie	122
Euphoria	58
Every so often one has to make a sound	10
Ferguson	19
Fern Rock	102

Fever	156
First Weekend	29
First, you will need to cross some dark threshold.	46
Flag of Imagination Furled, The	206
Flâneur Tends a Well-Liked Summer Cocktail, The	204
Forecast	162
For I was born, too, in the stunted winter of History.	135
Freddie Hubbard's playing the cassette deck	83
French Quarter, The	15
From the Liberty Bell's glass asylum,	52
Galaxy gowns	78
Going into Battle	205
Going to Meet the Man	137
Greek Revival	142
Gwen, I am glad you're not living at this hour,	126
Had I possessed the poise to kick	156
hand in hand remove our dark suits, but	201
Heaven Goes Online	152
Historians	40
Hoops	90
How to Avoid a Crash	245
How to Listen	82
How untouchable the girls arm-locked strutting	100
Hunting Park	118
I am bathing again, burying my face	219
I am going to cock my head tonight like a dog	82
I am revisiting the idea of Florida, giving my vertebrae	190
I am sure my grandfather would be ashamed	242
I am weary of light over Herring Cove,	118
I could give your palace more glass shine,	150
I could sit the rest of my life	7
I created a vacuum.	73
I emerge whenever he confuses the lamp for a moon.	251
If I told you Earl, the toughest kid	182

If you could listen to my thumbs	11
If you end your crusades for the great race,	22
I gave the bathtub purity and honor, and the sky	136
I Had the Craziest Dream	146
I have come to rely on the dark pilots	40
I have not disappeared.	180
I heard the terrible laughter of termites	63
I live on the roof of the world among the aerial	141
I'll Fly Away	80
I'll never forget the wind the corner whispered,	189
I'm best when I'm running full-throated	80
I'm glum about your sportive flesh in the empire of blab,	155
In cities overcoats turn everyone to philosophers.	37
Indian Song	83
In Memory of Derek Alton Walcott	227
In movies, the bad guy stands-off face	243
In Reading Market, you recall a fisherman in Sifnos	214
In the Eighties We Did the Wop	22
In the middle of March, the sky over Siena	206
In the solitary, shaded musk of a storefront	236
In this city no one talks dialectical materialism.	34
Invocation	26
I only know they want me, prone to stupefaction	144
I put a premium on rhymes—how could I	122
I remember the room in which he held	56
Island traffic slows to a halt	227
It doesn't matter if you can't see	61
It is wrong of me to speak ill of the whistle pig	31
It Must Be the Supermarket in Me	12
It must be the supermarket in me,	12
I thought by now my reverence would have waned,	234
I treasure any man who fashions his walk	42
I've Said Too Much	218
I've said too much. The soil overruns with honey.	218
Jane Says	144
Joyful Noise, A	73

Khanum, the things we did, 68

Language of the Moon 8
Late winter, sky darkening after school, 58
Leaving Saturn 70
Leave It All Up to Me 161
Let Me Begin Again 3
Let me begin again as a quiet thought 3
Life during Wartime 147
Like a sage walking a dirt road 241
Logan 110
Lorca in Eden 157
Lost Lake 145
Lovesick 46

Major and I 201
Making Things 4
Manna 153
Matthew Dickman and I are fond 232
Meeting People on Airplanes 41
Memories of West Fourth Street 33
Mighty Pawns 182
Migration 139
Mondes en Collision 138
Most Beautiful Man Never Performs Hard Labor, The 242
Most days I am full of spacious meadows, 14
Mr. Pate's Barbershop 56
My Children's Inheritance 211
My midway journey, my emancipated eyes 165
My Son and Me 216

Nashville Sonnet Deconstructed on a Bed of Magnolia Blossoms 34
Nature of Memory, The 28
Never on Sunday, she said and brandished 146
New Sphere of Influence 149
Night Steps 189
Nights withering into a forgery of chapels, 23

261

No one believes in angels.	249
North of Diamond Lake, the Cascades, crossmarks	55
Nothing to See Here, Move Along	250
Not that the white-aproned baker	41
November in Xichang	207
Now That You Are Here, I Can Think	248
Ocean You Answer To, The	5
Ode to Everything	39
Off from a double at McDonald's,	87
Of that unhurried blink of eyelids I glimpsed, all pixilated	142
Of Wolves and Imagination	10
Olney	106
Once again, I am trying to fall into the light,	28
Once there was a boy who thought it a noble idea	19
On Cocoa Beach	190
On Disappearing	180
One summer night I learned the art of	64
On Listening	11
Only a bearded smile shows below a conical hat	207
Only the skin runs ahead like a spruced-up	188
On the *Aegean Speed Line*, hightailing a fast ferry	168
On the *Manner of Addressing Shadows*	158
Oracle & Prophecy	244
Oregon Boogie	68
Our Eyes Are Far Away	246
Our eyes were far away, as were	246
Our social clock had gone berserk but those	148
Over and over again I bring the peach to my mouth,	45
Over powdered beignets,	15
Penn's *greene countrie towne* uncurled a shadow in the 19th century	50
Periplum	160
Pest	63
Picket Monsters	135
Pine shadows on snow like a Jasper canvas,	43

Plato would be easier, said the translator, and thus began	143
Poem with Borrowed Image from Marc Chagall	14
Practicing Kindness	31
Promise of Canonization, A	25
Reverse Voyage	165
Rock the Body Body	64
Romantics of Franconia Notch, The	232
Roof of the World	141
Said the Translator	143
Selling Out	87
Shall Inherit	17
She was light as a shadow. I wanted	151
Shouldering a bag of great literature, you glimpse spider silk	213
Skyrocketed—	70
So little to say of the iridescent grackles	18
Somehow, I have never thought	39
Some Kind of Crazy	61
Some mornings riding to work	245
So often I dream of the secrets of satellites	203
Sound We Dressed For, The	6
Special Needs	188
Spring Garden	130
Squat by a roadside near Eden, prairie flowers,	157
Stand Your Ground: A Double Golden Shovel	183
Suddenly I had to skewer all my prayers	4
Ten Album Covers	35
That moment in church when I stared at the reverend's black	101
That summer, municipality was on everyone's lips,	139
that were not ours though we understood their lives,	158
The birthmark on the lower right	205
The boughs have been naked for weeks.	221
The dead are a reservoir of secrets which they horde	44
The door I open to who I am is not a garage	154
The first time I got high I stood in a circle	60

The future is a blind piano man	35
The lake's cold shacks of ice-fishing anglers	237
The land nearly erased, the mountains flee.	239
The letter had not been sung	5
The mountains are at their theater again,	238
The notion that the land gave us flying	160
The roaring above rooftops riffed me out	235
The screen's fabrications remain. A film	140
The UN Somali driver speeds by a small herd	175
Think of Me, Laughing	21
Thinking in Swedish	7
Thinking of Our Shame at the Gas Pump	184
This is the year I'll contemplate the fire-fangled sky	149
Thoughts today	222
To the Makers	23
To the question of history's tectonic drift,	138
Towers	150
Treat the Flame	159
Urban Renewal	42, 49, 99, 168, 233
i. Night Museum	49
ii. Penn's *greene countrie towne* uncurled a shadow in the 19th century	50
iii. You are almost invisible in all this plain decay	31
iv. From the Liberty Bell's glass asylum	52
viii. Woofers stacked to pillars made a disco of a city block	53
ix. Bless your hallowed hands, Sir, and their paternal blues	54
xii. North of Diamond Lake, the Cascades, crossmarks	55
xvii. What of my fourth-grade teacher at Reynolds Elementary	99
xviii. How untouchable the girls arm-locked strutting	100
xix. That moment in church when I stared at the reverend's black	101
xxi. Greece	168
xxii. Spain	171
xxiii. Brazil	174
xxiv. Kenya	175

xxv. Italy	177
xxvi. Washington Square	233
xxvii. Thinking of Frost	234
xxviii. Paris	235
xxix. North Philadelphia	236
xxx. Fish & Wildlife	237
xxxi. Double View of the Adirondacks as Reflected over Lake Champlain from Waterfront Park	238
xxxii. The Valkyrie	239
lxxviii. I treasure any man who fashions his walk	42
lxxxi. Pine shadows on snow like a Jasper canvas	43
xciii. The dead are a reservoir of secrets which they horde	44
cxii. Over and over again I bring the peach to my mouth	45
Vermont Eclogue	220
We heard salvation	6
We were more than gestural, close-listening,	191
What if the wasteland is in us after all,	27
What I learned to endure was not the weight	244
What of my fourth-grade teacher at Reynolds Elementary,	99
What the heart knows: a ramekin	30
What you really are is svelte,	248
When all that cautions the eyes toward the imminent	233
When my toddler son recent of speech	29
When the sidewalk's eyes were weeping	152
When you have forgotten (to bring into	130
Whichever way our shoulders move, there's joy.	162
Why I Write Poetry	196
Why right now the iridescent blue of that bird	33
Why write to you? I cannot envision	106
Winter	221
Winter Eclogue	37
Wonderland Trail	24
Woofers stacked to pillars made a disco of a city block.	53
Writing birthed me	24
Wyoming	113

You are almost invisible in all this plain decay.	31
You, bow-shaped recipe of opulent whines	174
You could be home, boiling a pot	186
You, Reader	203
You're right to imagine me sobbing on the corner	21
Your own Social Aid & Pleasure	113

Also Available from
Major Jackson

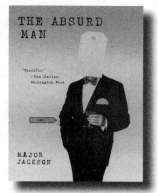

"Erudite. . . . [*The Absurd Man*] bring[s] us back to an existential truth that only poetry's fierce tenderness can offer."
—Sandra Simonds, *New York Times Book Review*

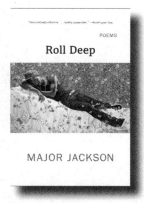

"This powerful book represents a painful but inspired journey."
—*Publishers Weekly*, starred review

"Devastatingly effective . . . lushly memorable."
—*Washington Post*

W. W. NORTON & COMPANY
Independent Publishers Since 1923